Downtown Basic

English for Work and Life

EDWARD J. MCBRIDE

HEINLE
CENGAGE Learning™

Australia • Brazil • Japan • Korea • Mexico • Singapore • Spain • United Kingdom • United States

HEINLE
CENGAGE Learning™

Downtown Basic: English for Work and Life
Edward J. McBride

Publisher: Sherrise Roehr

Acquisitions Editor: Tom Jefferies

Assistant Developmental Editor:
Cécile Engeln

Director of Content and Media Production:
Michael Burggren

Marketing Director, U.S.: Jim McDonough

Director of Adult Education Sales:
Eric Bredenberg

Marketing Communications Manager:
Beth Leonard

Senior Product Marketing Manager:
Katie Kelley

Senior Content Project Manager:
Maryellen Eschmann-Killeen

Senior Print Buyer: Mary Beth Hennebury

Developmental Editor: Kasia McNabb

Cover Design: Lori Stuart

Composition: Publication Services, Inc.

Library of Congress Control Number: 2008944056

ISBN-13: 978-1-4240-1656-3

ISBN-10: 1-4240-1656-8

Heinle
20 Channel Center Street
Boston, MA 02210
USA

Cengage Learning is a leading provider of customized learning solutions with office locations around the globe, including Singapore, the United Kingdom, Australia, Mexico, Brazil and Japan. Locate our local office at: **international.cengage.com/region**

Cengage Learning products are represented in Canada by Nelson Education, Ltd.

Visit Heinle online at **elt.heinle.com**
Visit our corporate website at **cengage.com**

Printed in the United States of America
1 2 3 4 5 6 7 8 9 10 11 10 09

Dedication

To all the wonderful students who have given me, over the years, at least as much as I have given them.

Acknowledgments

The author and publisher would like the thank the following reviewers for the valuable input:

Elizabeth Aderman
New York City Board of Education
New York, NY

Jolie Bechet
Fairfax Community Adult School
Los Angeles, CA

Cheryl Benz
Georgia Perimeter College
Clarkston, GA

Chan Bostwick
Los Angeles Unified School District
Los Angeles, CA

Patricia Brenner
University of Washington
Seattle, WA

Clif de Córdoba
Roosevelt Community Adult School
Los Angeles, CA

Marti Estrin
Santa Rosa Junior College
Santa Rosa, CA

Judith Finkelstein
Reseda Community Adult School
Reseda, CA

Lawrence Fish
Shorefront YM-YWHA
   English Language Program
Brooklyn, NY

Giang Hoang
Evans Community Adult School
Los Angeles, CA

Arther Hui
Mount San Antonio College
Walnut, CA

Renee Klosz
Lindsey Hopkins Technical
   Education Center
Miami, FL

Carol Lowther
Palomar College
San Marcos, CA

Barbara Oles
Literacy Volunteers of
   Greater Hartford
Hartford, CT

Pamela Rogers
Phoenix College
Phoenix, AZ

Eric Rosenbaum
BEGIN Managed Programs
New York, NY

Stan Yarbro
La Alianza Hispana
Roxbury, MA

Contents

Contents

EFF	CASAS	LAUSD Beginning Literacy & Beginning Low	Florida Foundations	Texas Level 1
Many EFF skills are practiced in this chapter, with a particular focus on: • Learn Through Research • Convey Ideas in Writing • Speak So Others Can Understand • Listen Actively • Cooperate With Others	**Lesson 1:** 0.1.4, 0.1.5, 0.1.6, 0.2.1	**Beginning Literacy Competencies:** 1a, 1b, 1c, 2, 3a, 3b, 4b, 4d, 5d, 5e, 5k, 5l **Grammar:** 1a, 4f, 5c, 5d, 8c	**Lesson 1:** 1.01.01, 1.01.02	**Lesson 1:** • **Speaking:** 1.1, 2.1, 3.1, 4.1 • **Listening:** 1.1, 2.1, 3.1, 4.1 • **Reading:** 2.1, 3.1, 5.1, 6.1 • **Writing:** 1.1, 2.1, 3.1, 4.1, 5.1
	Lesson 2: 0.1.2, 0.1.4, 0.1.5, 0.1.6, 0.2.1, 6.0.1, 6.0.2	**Beginning Low Competencies:** 1, 2, 4, 5, 7, 9a, 9b, 11a, 11b, 58a, 58b, 60 **Grammar:** 1a, 10c, 11a, 11b	**Lesson 2:** 1.01.02, 1.04.01	**Lesson 2:** • **Speaking:** 1.1, 2.1, 3.1, 4.1 • **Listening:** 1.1, 2.1, 3.1, 4.1, 5.1 • **Reading:** 1.1, 2.1, 3.1, 5.1, 6.1 • **Writing:** 1.1, 2.1, 3.1, 4.1, 5.1
	Lesson 3: 0.1.2, 0.1.4, 0.1.5, 0.2.1, 0.2.2, 2.8.5, 7.2.1		**Lesson 3:** 1.01.02, 1.04.01	**Lesson 3:** **Speaking:** 1.1, 2.1, 3.1, 4.1 • **Listening:** 1.1, 2.1, 3.1 • **Reading:** 1.1, 2.1, 3.1, 5.1 • **Writing:** 1.1, 2.1, 3.1, 4.1, 5.1
Many EFF skills are practiced in this chapter, with a particular focus on: • Learn Through Research • Speak So Others Can Understand • Listen Actively • Guide Others	**Lesson 1:** 0.1.1, 0.1.2, 0.1.5, 0.1.6	**Beginning Literacy Competencies:** 4b, 4d, 5f, 5g, 5h, 5k, 5l, 5m, 7, 8a, 8b, 8c, 9 **Grammar:** 1a, 1b, 2, 4a, 4b, 4c, 5b, 6c, 7c, 8a, 11a, 11c	**Lesson 1:** 1.01.04	**Lesson 1:** • **Speaking:** 2.1, 3.1, 4.1 • **Listening:** 1.1, 2.1, 3.1 • **Reading:** 2.1, 3.1, 6.1 • **Writing:** 1.1, 3.1, 4.1, 5.1
	Lesson 2: 0.1.2, 0.1.4, 0.1.5, 2.2.1, 2.8.3	**Beginning Low Competencies:** 2, 4, 8, 9a, 9b, 9c, 12, 15, 16, 17, 18, 60 **Grammar:** 1a, 5, 9a, 9b, 9c, 9d, 10b, 11a, 12a, 14a, 16a, 16ci, 16cii	**Lesson 2:** 1.01.03, 1.06.03	**Lesson 2:** • **Speaking:** 1.1, 2.1, 4.1 • **Listening:** 2.1, 3.1, 5.1 • **Reading:** 2.1, 3.1, 4.1, 5.1, 6.1 • **Writing:** 1.1, 3.1, 4.1, 5.1
	Lesson 3: 0.1.2, 0.1.4, 0.1.5, 0.1.7, 0.1.8, 0.2.1, 2.4.1		**Lesson 3:** 1.01.01, 1.01.02, 1.01.04, 1.02.10	**Lesson 3:** • **Speaking:** 1.1., 2.1, 3.1, 4.1 • **Listening:** 1.1, 2.1, 3.1, 5.1 • **Reading:** 1.1, 2.1, 3.1, 5.1 • **Writing:** 1.1, 2.1, 3.1, 4.1, 5.1

Contents

Contents

EFF	CASAS	LAUSD Beginning Literacy & Beginning Low	Florida Foundations	Texas Level 1
Many EFF skills are practiced in this chapter, with a particular focus on: • Take Responsibility for Learning • Reflect and Evaluate • Learn Through Research • Read With Understanding • Convey Ideas in Writing • Speak So Others Can Understand • Listen Actively	**Lesson 1:** 0.1.2, 0.1.5, 0.1.6, 2.3.1, 2.3.3, 4.4.1, 6.6.4 **Lesson 2:** 0.1.2, 0.1.5, 0.1.6, 0.2.4, 2.3.2, 2.8.3, 3.1.2 **Lesson 3:** 0.1.2, 0.1.5, 0.1.6, 0.2.1, 1.2.1, 2.3.2, 2.3.4, 2.7.1, 7.2.1	**Beginning Literacy Competencies:** 1b, 4a, 4b, 4d, 5k, 6a, 6b, 6c, 6d **Grammar:** 1c, 1d, 1f, 4d, 5e, 7a, 8b, 9, 11c **Beginning Low Competencies:** 3, 11a, 11b, 13, 25, 26, 27, 28, 29, 40, 55, 60 **Grammar:** 1a, 9c, 13a, 14c, 16a, 16ci, 16ciii	**Lesson 1:** 1.03.09, 1.02.05 **Lesson 2:** 1.01.03, 1.01.05, 1.03.10 **Lesson 3:** 1.01.03, 1.01.05, 1.02.03, 1.03.10, 1.04.01	**Lesson 1:** • **Speaking:** 1.1, 2.1, 4.1 • **Listening:** 1.1, 2.1, 3.1, 4.1, 5.1 • **Reading:** 1.1, 2.1, 3.1 • **Writing:** 1.1, 2.1, 3.1, 4.1, 5.1 **Lesson 2:** • **Speaking:** 1.1., 2.1, 3.1, 4.1 • **Listening:** 1.1, 2.1, 3.1, 4.1 • **Reading:** 1.1, 2.1, 3.1, 5.1, 6.1 • **Writing:** 1.1, 2.1, 3.1, 4.1, 5.1 **Lesson 3:** • **Speaking:** 1.1., 2.1, 3.1, 4.1 • **Listening:** 1.1, 2.1, 3.1, 4.1, 5.1 • **Reading:** 1.1, 2.1, 3.1, 5.1, 6.1 • **Writing:** 1.1, 2.1, 3.1, 4.1, 5.1
Many EFF skills are practiced in this chapter, with a particular focus on: • Reflect and Evaluate • Read With Understanding • Speak So Others Can Understand • Use Math to Solve Problems and Make Decisions • Guide Others	**Lesson 1:** 0.1.2, 0.1.5, 0.1.6, 1.1.6, 1.2.1, 1.2.9, 1.3.1, 1.8.6, 6.0.2 **Lesson 2:** 0.1.2, 0.1.5, 0.1.6, 1.2.1, 1.2.9 **Lesson 3:** 0.1.2, 0.1.5, 0.1.6, 1.2.1, 1.2.9, 1.3.1, 1.6.4	**Beginning Literacy Competencies:** 1b, 4b, 4d, 5d, 7, 8a, 8b, 8c, 12, 13, 14, 15 **Grammar:** 1a, 4b, 4c, 6a, 7b, 11a, 11c, 13 **Beginning Low Competencies:** 11a, 14a, 30a, 31, 33, 34, 60 **Grammar:** 1b, 9b, 11a, 12b, 16cii, 17, 19	**Lesson 1:** 1.04.02, 1.04.06, 1.04.08 **Lesson 2:** 1.01.03, 1.04.03 **Lesson 3:** 1.01.03, 1.04.02, 1.04.03, 1.04.06, 1.04.07	**Lesson 1:** • **Speaking:** 1.1, 2.1, 3.1, 4.1 • **Listening:** 1.1, 2.1, 3.1, 4.1, 5.1 • **Reading:** 1.1, 2.1, 3.1, 6.1 • **Writing:** 1.1, 2.1, 3.1, 4.1, 5.1 **Lesson 2:** • **Speaking:** 1.1, 2.1, 3.1, 4.1 • **Listening:** 1.1, 2.1, 3.1, 5.1 • **Reading:** 2.1, 3.1, 6.1 • **Writing:** 1.1, 2.1, 3.1, 4.1, 5.1 **Lesson 3:** • **Speaking:** 1.1, 2.1, 3.1, 4.1 • **Listening:** 1.1, 2.1, 3.1, 5.1 • **Reading:** 2.1, 3.1, 6.1 • **Writing:** 1.1, 3.1, 4.1, 5.1

Contents

EFF	CASAS	LAUSD Beginning Literacy & Beginning Low	Florida Foundations	Texas Level 1
Many EFF skills are practiced in this chapter, with a particular focus on: • Convey Ideas in Writing • Speak So Others Can Understand • Listen Actively • Cooperate With Others	**Lesson 1:** 0.1.1, 0.1.2, 0.1.4, 0.1.5, 0.1.6, 0.2.1, 0.2.2	**Beginning Literacy Competencies:** 1a, 1b, 1d, 1e, 2, 3, 4b, 4d, 6a **Grammar:** 1a, 1g, 4b, 4d, 6b, 11a, 11c, 13	**Lesson 1:** 1.01.02, 1.01.03, 1.02.07	**Lesson 1:** • **Speaking:** 1.1, 2.1, 4.1 • **Listening:** 1.1, 2.1, 3.1, 4.1, 5.1 • **Reading:** 2.1, 3.1, 5.1 • **Writing:** 1.1, 3.1, 4.1, 5.1
	Lesson 2: 0.1.2, 0.1.5, 0.2.4, 1.4.1, 2.3.1, 7.2.1, 8.1.1, 8.1.2, 8.1.3, 8.2.1, 8.2.2	**Beginning Low Competencies:** 1, 3, 6, 7, 9b, 11b, 12, 13, 25 38, 51, 60 **Grammar:** 2, 9c, 12a, 12b, 16ci, 19	**Lesson 2:** 1.03.09	**Lesson 2:** • **Speaking:** 2.1, 4.1 • **Listening:** 1.1, 2.1, 3.1 • **Reading:** 2.1, 3.1 , 6.1 • **Writing:** 1.1, 3.1, 4.1, 5.1
	Lesson 3: 0.1.2, 0.1.5, 0.1.6, 4.1.8, 8.1.1, 8.1.3		**Lesson 3:** 1.03.01	**Lesson 3:** • **Speaking:** 2.1, 4.1 • **Listening:** 1.1, 2.1, 3.1 • **Reading:** 2.1, 3.1, • **Writing:** 1.1, 2.1, 3.1, 5.1
Many EFF skills are practiced in this chapter, with a particular focus on: • Reflect and Evaluate • Speak So Others Can Understand	**Lesson 1:** 0.1.2, 0.1.5, 1.4.1	**Beginning Literacy Competencies:** 4b, 4d, 5d, 5f, 5h, 5k **Grammar:** 1a, 5a, 6, 8a, 10, 11a, 11b, 11c	**Lesson 1:** 1.06.03	**Lesson 1:** • **Speaking:** 2.1, 4.1 • **Listening:** 1.1, 2.1, 3.1 • **Reading:** 2.1, 3.1 • **Writing:** 1.1, 2.1, 3.1, 4.1, 5.1
	Lesson 2: 0.1.2, 0.1.5, 0.1.6, 1.2.1, 1.4.1, 1.4.7, 7.2.3, 8.2.6	**Beginning Low Competencies:** 2, 11a, 31, 38, 39, 60 **Grammar:** 10a, 12a, 13b, 14a, 16b, 16cii, 19	**Lesson 2:** 1.04.02, 1.04.04, 1.04.06	**Lesson 2:** • **Speaking:** 2.1, 4.1 • **Listening:** 1.1, 2.1, 3.1, 5.1 • **Reading:** 2.1, 3.1 • **Writing:** 1.1, 2.1, 3.1, 4.1, 5.1
	Lesson 3: 0.1.2, 0.1.5, 1.4.1, 1.4.2, 1.4.4, 7.2.3		**Lesson 3:** 1.04.04, 1.04.05	**Lesson 3:** • **Speaking:** 2.1, 3.1, 4.1 • **Listening:** 1.1, 2.1, 3.1, 5.1 • **Reading:** 1.1, 2.1, 3.1, 4.1 • **Writing:** 1.1, 2.1, 3.1, 4.1, 5.1
Many EFF skills are practiced in this chapter, with a particular focus on: • Reflect and Evaluate • Learn Through Research • Convey Ideas in Writing • Speak So Others Can Understand • Listen Actively • Observe Critically	**Lesson 1:** 0.1.2, 0.1.5, 0.1.6, 2.2.1, 2.2.5	**Beginning Literacy Competencies:** 4a, 4b, 4d **Grammar:** 2, 5a, 8a, 10, 11a, 11c,	**Lesson 1:** 1.02.01, 1.02.02, 1.04.09, 1.06.03	**Lesson 1:** • **Speaking:** 1.1, 2.1, 3.1, 4.1 • **Listening:** 1.1, 2.1, 3.1 • **Reading:** 2.1, 3.1, 4.1, 5.1, 6.1 • **Writing:** 1.1, 2.1, 3.1 4.1, 5.1
	Lesson 2: 0.1.2, 0.1.5, 0.1.6, 1.2.6, 1.8.1, 2.2.1, 2.2.2, 2.2.3, 2.2.5, 2.4.4, 7.2.1	**Beginning Low Competencies:** 11b, 22, 23a, 23b, 24a, 24b, 50, 51, 60 **Grammar:** 1a, 1b, 3, 5, 7, 14a, 10a, 10e, 16ciii	**Lesson 2:** 1.02.01, 1.02.02, 1.02.10, 1.04.06, 1.04.09, 1.06.01, 1.06.02, 1.06.03	**Lesson 2:** • **Speaking:** 1.1, 2.1, 3.1, 4.1 • **Listening:** 1.1, 2.1, 3.1, 5.1 • **Reading:** 1.1, 2.1, 3.1, 4.1, 5.1, 6.1 • **Writing:** 1.1, 2.1, 3.1 4.1, 5.1
	Lesson 3: 0.1.2, 0.1.5, 0.1.6, 0.2.4, 4.1.8, 7.2.1		**Lesson 3:** 1.03.01, 1.03.06	**Lesson 3:** • **Speaking:** 2.1, 3.1, 4.1 • **Listening:** 2.1, 3.1, 5.1 • **Reading:** 2.1, 3.1 • **Writing:** 1.1, 2.1, 3.1 4.1, 5.1

Contents

Contents

From the Author . . .

Learning a new language can be challenging, and even, sometimes, frustrating. But learning English should also be fun. That's the idea I was given by the wonderful administrator who hired me twelve years ago to teach my first ESL class. She took me aside as I was about to walk nervously into class for the first time. "Make your students comfortable," she said. "Make the class fun. And teach them what they really need to know."

Twelve years of teaching and thousands of students later, these simple, yet essential ideas have become guiding pedagogical principles for me. In my classes, I strive to teach students what they need to know, in a way that is both comfortable and enjoyable. Ultimately that's the philosophy behind *Downtown*, too. The simplicity of the layout, along with the logical, paced progression of the material makes it a comfortable text for both teachers and students to use. The wide variety of activities, including playful features like "Game Time" and the *Downtown* Cartoon make *Downtown* enjoyable to use. And, by developing the text with a focus on standards-based competencies, *Downtown* teaches students the information they most need to know.

This five-level, competency-based series is built around the language skills students need to function in both their every day lives and in the workplace, while giving a good deal of attention to grammar as well. It is a general ESL text that pays more attention to work-related language needs than is typical. The goal is to facilitate student centered learning, leading students to real communicative competence.

The first page of each chapter presents an overview of the material to be covered, in context, through a picture dictionary. This is followed by three lessons, with the third lesson focusing on work-related English. Many of the structures and key concepts are recycled throughout the lessons to maximize student practice. Each lesson is carefully scaffolded to progress from guided practice to more communicative activities in which students take more control of their learning.

Each chapter concludes with a Review lesson which practices and synthesizes the skills and grammar learned in the previous three lessons. The review culminates in a "Teamwork Task." This gives students the opportunity to work together to apply the skills they have learned to complete a real world type of task. At the end of each chapter is a humorous cartoon story which invites students to practice the vocabulary and grammar learned in the chapter.

Each chapter presents a variety of activities which practice grammar, reading, writing, listening, and speaking skills. Problem solving activities are also included, and are particularly emphasized at the higher levels. The material in *Downtown* is presented in real life contexts. Students are introduced to vocabulary, grammar, and real world skills through the interactions of a cast of realistic, multi-ethnic characters who function as parents, workers and community members in their own "downtown" world.

My intention in developing *Downtown* was to provide you with an easy-to-use text, brimming with essential and enjoyable language learning material. I hope *Downtown* helps to cultivate an effective and motivating learning atmosphere in your classroom.

Photo Credits

Frontmatter

Page xvii: Top left: © Jupiterimages/BananaStock/Alamy; Top center left: © Tony Metaxas/Getty Images; Left center: © Jose Luis Pelaez Inc./Photolibrary; Bottom center left: © Chris Rout/Alamy; Bottom left: © Jack Hollingsworth/Getty Images; Top right: © Ariel Skelley/Getty Images; Top center right: © Zubin Schroff/Getty Images; Bottom center right: © Blend Images/Alamy; Bottom right: © RK Studio/Getty Images

Chapter 1

Page 4: Bottom: © Mark Hunt/Photolibrary

Page 14: Left: © Shannon Fagan/Getty Images; Left center: © Brooke Fasani/Getty Images; Right center: © Jupiterimages; Right: © Ingram Publishing (Superstock Limited)/Alamy

Chapter 2

Page 25: Top left: © Andy Crawford/Getty Images; Top center: © Sharpshot/Dreamstime.com; Top right: © Tamilsma/Dreamstime.com; Bottom left: © Margojh/Dreamstime.com; Bottom center: © Oktay Ortakcioglu/iStockPhoto; Bottom right: © Ronen/Shutterstock

Page 26: Top left: © Oliver Blondeau/iStockPhoto; Top right: © Boroda/Dreamstime.com; Top center left: © Cfan/Dreamstime.com; Top center right: © Atman/Dreamstime.com; Bottom center left: © Georgios/Dreamstime.com; Bottom center right: © Dorling Kindersley/Getty Images; Bottom left: © Elnur/Shutterstock; Bottom right: © Margojh/Dreamstime.com

Page 27: Top left: © Jcphoto/Dreamstime.com; Top right: © Chasbrutland/Dreamstime.com; Bottom left: © Vinivecoso/Dreamstime.com; Bottom center: © Margojh/Dreamstime.com; Bottom right: © Spauln/Dreamstime.com; © Malcom Leman/Shutterstock

Page 28: Left: © Nancy Brown/Getty Images; Center: © Jon Feingersh/Getty Images; Right: © Doug MacLellan/Alamy;

Chapter 3

Page 54: Top: © Tony Metaxas/Getty Images; Bottom left: © Jupiterimages/BananaStock/Alamy; Right: © Zubin Schroff/Getty Images

Chapter 4

Page 64: © Kaspars Grinvalds/Shutterstock; © Stillfx/Dreamstime.com; © Klikk/Dreamstime.com; © Stillfx/Dreamstime.com; © Mosich/Dreamstime.com; © Njnightsky/Dreamstime.com; © Njnightsky/Dreamstime.com; © Njnightsky/Dreamstime.com; © Asiavasmund/Dreamstime.com

Page 65: © Aberenyi/Dreamstime.com; © Kaspars Grinvalds/Shutterstock; © Stillfx/Dreamstime.com; © Klikk/Dreamstime.com; © Njnightsky/Dreamstime.com; © Njnightsky/Dreamstime.com; © Asiavasmund/Dreamstime.com

Chapter 6

Page 104: Top: © Hanhanpegg/Dreamstime.com; Center left: © Crodenberg/Dreamstime.com; Center right: © Mamahoohoo/Dreamstime.com; Bottom left: © Redking/Dreamstime.com; Bottom right: © Liane Cary/Photolibrary

Page 105: Top: © Sklepspozy/Dreamstime.com; Center left: © Icewind78/Dreamstime.com; Top center: © Debljames/Dreamstime.com; Center right: © Phartisan/Dreamstime.com; Bottom left: © ML Harris/Getty Images; Bottom center: © Zbieg2001/Dreamstime.com; Bottom right: © Addict/Dreamstime.com

Page 106: Top: © Mitchellb/Dreamstime.com; Bottom left: © Sgtrockin/Dreamstime.com; Bottom center: © Crodenberg/Dreamstime.com; Bottom right: © Michael Grimm/Getty Images

Page 113: Top left: © Frick Byers/Getty Images; Top right: © Simon Marcus/Photolibrary; Bottom left: © Delion/Dreamstime.com; Bottom right: © Jonasbsl/Dreamstime.com

Chapter 7

Page 130: Left: © Clark, Bruce/Jupiterimages; Right: © Barry Winiker/Photolibrary

Page 134: Top: © Andresr/Dreamstime.com; Bottom: © Tugores34/Dreamstime.com

Chapter 8

Page 154: Top: © Thecult/Dreamstime.com; Bottom Left: © Justinjohn…/Dreamstime.com; Bottom right: © Roy Morsch/Photolibrary

Chapter 9

Page 175: Top left: © Jeff Zaruba/Getty Images; Top center: © iStockPhoto; Top center: © iStockPhoto; Top right: © Andy Whale/Getty Images; Bottom left: © Serdar Yagci/iStockPhoto; Bottom center: © Romilly Lockyer/Getty Images; Bottom right: © Rachel Watson/Getty Images

Chapter 10

Page 187: Top: © Dorling Kindersley/Getty Images; Bottom left: © Jupiterimages; Bottom center: © Scott Simms/Jupiterimages; Bottom right: © Howard Deshong/Getty Images

Downtown: English for Work and Life

Downtown offers a well-balanced approach that combines a standards-based and a grammar-based syllabus. This gives English learners the comprehensive language skills they need to succeed in their daily lives, both at home and at work.

- **Picture dictionary-style chapter openers** introduce vocabulary in context and outline chapter goals.

- **Audio CDs** enhance learning through dialogues, listening practice, readings, and pronunciation exercises.

Theme-based chapters include three lessons. The third lesson in each chapter focuses on skills and vocabulary necessary for the workplace.

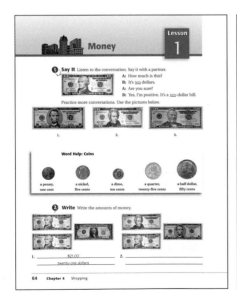

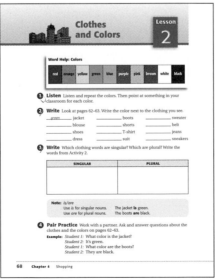

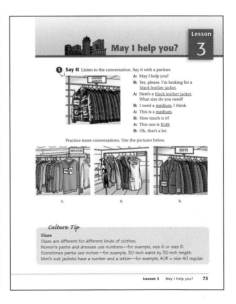

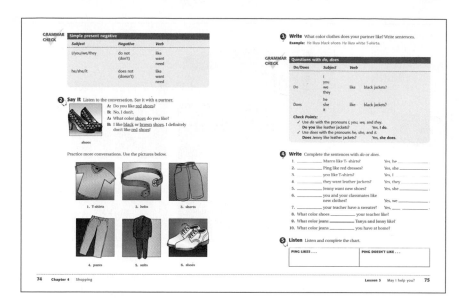

- **The strong grammar syllabus** supports the integrated language learning focus.

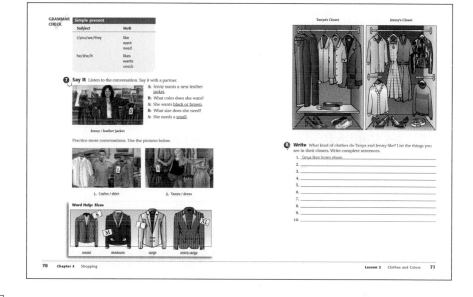

- **The lives of recurring characters provide the context** for a variety of activities such as *Grammar Check, Say It, Game Time,* and other communicative items.

- **Problem solving activities** engage students' critical thinking.

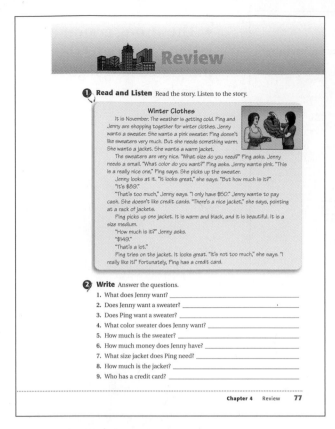

• **Review pages** practice all skills learned in the chapter and let students synthesize what they have learned.

• **A comic book story** at the end of each chapter reviews instructional content while providing the basis for role-play and team tasks.

Downtown Components

Audio CDs enhance learning through dialogues, listening practice, readings, and pronunciation exercises.

Workbooks reinforce lessons and maximize student practice of key reading, writing, listening, speaking, and grammar points.

Transparencies can be used to introduce lessons, develop vocabulary, and stimulate expansion activities.

Assessment CD-ROM with *ExamView®* allows teachers to create, customize, and correct tests and quizzes quickly and easily.

Teacher's Editions provide student book answers and teaching suggestions.

Alignment with the CASAS, SCANS, EFF Competencies and state standards supports classroom and program goals.

Characters in *Downtown Basic*

Alison is an English teacher at the Downtown Adult School. She is from the United States.

Alison Ryan

Ping is a student at the Downtown Adult School. She is from China.

Ping Chang

Marco is a student at the Downtown Adult School. He is from Mexico. Hc is a cook.

Marco Lopez

Tanya is a student at the Downtown Adult School, in Alison's class. She is from Russia. She is a hair stylist.

Tanya Ivanova

Carlos is a student at the Downtown Adult School, in Alison's class. He is from El Salvador. He is a mechanic.

Carlos Garcia

Jenny is a student at the Downtown Adult School. She is from Colombia. She works at a café.

Jenny Vidal

Han is a student at the Downtown Adult School. He is from Vietnam. He is a house painter, but wants to work in an office.

Han Do

Monica is a student at the Downtown Adult School. She is from Brazil. She wants to be a teacher's assistant.

Monica Silva

Julia is a student at the Downtown Adult School. She is from Haiti. She is a salesperson.

Julia Charles

Names and Numbers

GOALS

- ✓ Identify and write the letters of the alphabet.
- ✓ Introduce yourself.
- ✓ Ask for and tell names.
- ✓ Spell your name.
- ✓ Identify and write numbers.
- ✓ Ask for and tell addresses.
- ✓ Ask for and tell phone numbers.
- ✓ Ask for and tell native countries and languages.
- ✓ Complete a registration form.
- ✓ Identify and use the verb *be*.
- ✓ Identify and use personal pronouns.
- ✓ Identify and use possessive adjectives.

On the chalkboard:

ABCD_FG_IJ_LMN
O_QRSTU_WXYZ

I AM YOUR TEACHER.
MY FIRST NAME IS ALISON.
WHAT'S YOUR FIRST NAME?

Name cards: Alison Ryan · Carlos, El Salvador

1 Listen Listen and repeat.

A ____	a ____
B ____	b ____
C ____	c ____
D ____	d ____
E ____	e ____
F ____	f ____
G ____	g ____
H ____	h ____
I ____	i ____
J ____	j ____
K ____	k ____
L ____	l ____
M ____	m ____
N ____	n ____
O ____	o ____
P ____	p ____
Q ____	q ____
R ____	r ____
S ____	s ____
T ____	t ____
U ____	u ____
V ____	v ____
W ____	w ____
X ____	x ____
Y ____	y ____
Z ____	z ____

2 Write Write the letters. Then write the missing letters in the picture.

Names

Lesson 1

1 Say It Listen to the conversation. Say it with your teacher. Use your name.

A: Hello. I am your teacher. My name is <u>Alison Ryan</u>.

B: Hello. My name is <u>Ping Chang</u>.

A: Nice to meet you, <u>Ping</u>.

B: Nice to meet you, too.

2 Pair Practice Practice the conversation with a partner.

A: Hello. I am your classmate. My name is _____.

B: Hi. My name is _____.

A: Nice to meet you, _____.

B: Nice to meet you, too.

3 Group Practice Stand up and introduce yourself to five classmates.

4 **Write** Make a name card. Put it on your desk.

My name is
Alison Ryan
(first name)   (last name)

5 **Pronunciation** Listen and repeat.

A a   E e   I i   O o   U u   Y y

6 **Listen** Listen. Circle the letter you hear.

1. (A)   E   6. i   y
2. I   E   7. a   y
3. E   Y   8. u   w
4. A   I   9. i   a
5. O   U   10. e   a

7 **Listen** Listen. Write the missing letters.

1. My first name is   2. My last name is   3. My full name is
   T _ N _ A.   L _ P _ _ .   M _ N _ C A
                                                        S _ L _ A.

4 **Write** Make a name card. Put it on your desk.

8 Say It Listen to the conversation. Say it with a partner.

A: Hello. My name is <u>Han Do</u>.

B: I'm sorry. What's your first name?

A: <u>Han. H-A-N</u>.

B: Nice to meet you, <u>Han</u>. I am <u>Tanya</u>.

A: Nice to meet you, too, <u>Tanya</u>.

Han / Tanya

9 Pair Practice Practice the conversation with a partner.

A: Hello. My name is ＿＿＿＿＿＿ ＿＿＿＿＿＿.

B: I'm sorry. What's your first name?

A: My first name is ＿＿＿＿＿. ＿ ＿ ＿ ＿ ＿. (Spell your first name.)

B: Nice to meet you, ＿＿＿＿＿. I am ＿＿＿＿＿.

A: Nice to meet you, too, ＿＿＿＿＿.

10 Write Complete the sentences with words from the boxes.

1. My ＿＿＿＿＿ name is Alison.

   My last ＿＿＿＿＿ is Ryan.

   What's ＿＿＿＿＿ first name?

   | name |
   | your |
   | first |

2. **A:** ＿＿＿＿＿ first name is Monica.

   B: Nice to ＿＿＿＿＿ you, Monica.

   A: Nice to meet ＿＿＿＿＿, too.

   | you |
   | meet |
   | My |

11 **Teamwork Task** Sit in a group of four or five students. Ask your classmates their names. Write their names.

> **Example:** *Student 1:* What's your first name?
> *Student 2:* Tanya. T-A-N-Y-A.
> *Student 1:* And your last name?

My Classmates

First Name	Last Name

Game Time

Bingo

Write a letter in each box. Listen to your teacher. Circle the letters you hear. Say **Bingo** when you circle three letters in a row. Read your letters to your teacher.

Make another bingo card and play again!

Numbers

1. Listen Listen and repeat the numbers.

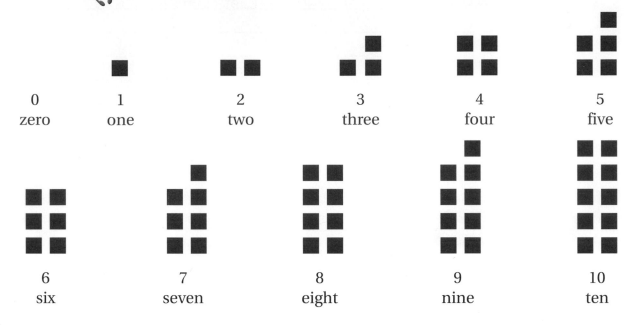

0	1	2	3	4	5
zero	one	two	three	four	five

6	7	8	9	10
six	seven	eight	nine	ten

11	12	13	14	15	16	17	18	19
eleven	twelve	thirteen	fourteen	fifteen	sixteen	seventeen	eighteen	nineteen

20	30	40	50	60	70	80	90	100
twenty	thirty	forty	fifty	sixty	seventy	eighty	ninety	one hundred

2. Pronunciation Listen and repeat the numbers.

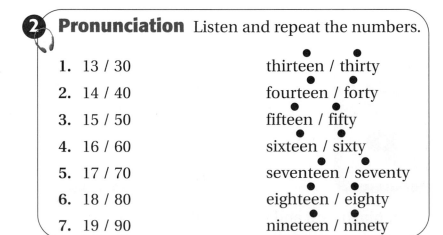

1. 13 / 30   thirteen / thirty
2. 14 / 40   fourteen / forty
3. 15 / 50   fifteen / fifty
4. 16 / 60   sixteen / sixty
5. 17 / 70   seventeen / seventy
6. 18 / 80   eighteen / eighty
7. 19 / 90   nineteen / ninety

3 **Say It** Listen to the conversation. Say it with a partner.

A: What is your telephone number?

B: My telephone number?

A: Yes.

B: My area code is <u>eight, one, eight</u>.

A: And the phone number?

B: My phone number is <u>five, five, five—three, two, three, zero</u>.

Practice more conversations. Use the pictures below.

1.

2.

4 **Listen** Listen and circle the number you hear.

1.	13	(30)	5.	7	17
2.	18	80	6.	6	60
3.	14	40	7.	90	19
4.	16	60	8.	50	15

5 **Write** Write your phone number.

1. My area code is _____ .

2. My phone number is _____ .

6 Say It Listen to the conversations. Say them with a partner.

(818) 555-9850

His

A: What is <u>his</u> telephone number?

B: <u>His</u> area code is <u>eight, one, eight</u>.

A: And <u>his</u> phone number?

B: <u>His</u> phone number is <u>five, five, five-nine, eight, five, zero</u>.

(310) 555-8513

Her

A: What is <u>her</u> telephone number?

B: <u>Her</u> area code is <u>three, one, zero</u>.

A: And <u>her</u> phone number?

B: <u>Her</u> phone number is <u>five, five, five-eight, five, one, three</u>.

Practice more conversations. Use the pictures below.

(213) 555-6718

1. **Her**

(310) 555-5670

2. **His**

Note: Say your phone number: (818) 555-5670
In the U.S., say your phone number like this:
eight, one, eight—five, five, five—five, six, seven, zero, *OR*
eight, one, eight—five, five, five—fifty-six, seventy

Say It Listen to the conversation. Say it with a partner.

A: What's your address?

B: My address is <u>324</u> <u>Rose Avenue</u>.

A: How do you spell that?

B: <u>Rose, R-O-S-E, Avenue</u>.

A: Thank you.

B: You're welcome.

Practice more conversations. Use the pictures below.

1.

2.

3

Word Help: Abbreviations

Ave. = Avenue   Blvd. = Boulevard

Rd. = Road   St. = Street   Apt. = Apartment

Listen Listen and write the missing numbers.

1. My address is ____ ____ ____ Avenue A.

2. My phone number is (213) ____ ____ ____ -65 ____ ____.

3. His area code is ____ ____ ____. His phone number is
   555 - ____ ____ ____ ____.

4. Her address is ____ ____ ____ ____ Rose Avenue. Her apartment
   number is _____.

5. Their phone number is (415) ____ ____ ____ - ____ ____ ____ ____.

9 Teamwork Task Work in teams of four.

A. Ask your teammates for their name, address, area code, and phone number. Write their answers.

Ask: *What is your first name? What is your address? What is your area code? What is your phone number?*

NAME	ADDRESS	AREA CODE	PHONE NUMBER

B. Tell your teacher about one of your teammates.

Game Time

Bingo
Write a number in each box (1–20, 30, 40, 50, 60, 70, 80, 90, 100). Listen to your teacher. Circle the numbers you hear. Say **Bingo** when you circle three numbers in a row. Read your numbers to your teacher.

Make another bingo card and play again.

Where are you from?

1 **Say It** Listen to the conversation. Say it with a partner.

A: Who is <u>she</u>?

B: <u>She</u> is my classmate. <u>Her</u> name is Ping.

A: Where is <u>she</u> from?

B: <u>She</u> is from <u>China</u>.

She / Her

Practice more conversations. Use the pictures below.

1. She / Her

2. He / His

3. She / Her

4. He / His

GRAMMAR CHECK

Subject pronouns / Possessive adjectives	
Subject pronouns	**Possessive adjectives**
I am from China.	**My** name is Ping.
You are from Russia.	**Your** name is Tanya.
He is from Vietnam.	**His** name is Han.
She is from Brazil.	**Her** name is Monica.
We are from Mexico.	**Our** names are Marco and Carolina.
They are from New York.	**Their** names are Eric and Alison.

2 Say It Listen to the conversation. Say it with a partner.

Mexico / Spanish

A: Who are they?

B: They are my classmates.

A: Where are they from?

B: They are from <u>Mexico</u>. Their native language is <u>Spanish</u>.

Practice more conversations. Use the pictures below.

1. **China / Chinese**

2. **Haiti / French**

3. **Iran / Farsi**

4. **Japan / Japanese**

3 Match Match the country with the language.

<u>c</u> 1. Korea   **a.** Russian

_____ 2. Spain   **b.** French

_____ 3. Brazil   **c.** Korean

_____ 4. Russia   **d.** Spanish

_____ 5. France   **e.** Portuguese

GRAMMAR CHECK

Contractions of *be*	
Complete verb	***Contraction***
I am from Mexico.	**I'm** from Mexico.
You are from China.	**You're** from China.
He is my classmate.	**He's** my classmate.
She is a teacher.	**She's** a teacher.
It is my telephone number.	**It's** my telephone number.
We are students.	**We're** students.
They are from Mexico.	**They're** from Mexico.

Check Point:

✓ Use contractions for questions, too.

What is = What's

4 Pronunciation Listen and repeat the contractions.

I'm	*I'm* a teacher.
You're	*You're* a student.
He's	*He's* my classmate.
She's	*She's* from Mexico.
It's	*It's* my telephone number.
We're	*We're* from Brazil.
They're	*They're* students.

5 Write Complete the sentences with contractions or complete verbs.

1. She is from Mexico.   ___She's___ from Mexico.

2. They are my classmates.   _____ my classmates.

3. We are from China.   _____ from China.

4. It is my native language.   _____ my native language.

5. I am a student.   _____ a student.

6. Alison _____ my teacher.   She's my teacher.

7. We _____ from Iran.   We're from Iran.

8. I _____ from Japan.   I'm from Japan.

6 Group Practice Work with a large group or with the whole class. Walk around the room. Ask your classmates questions. Write in the chart.

Ask: *What's your first name? Where are you from? What's your native language?*

NAME	COUNTRY	NATIVE LANGUAGE
Jenny	Colombia	Spanish

7 **Write** Answer the questions about the student registration form.

```
┌─────────────────────────────────────────────────────────┐
│  (D)  STUDENT REGISTRATION FORM  (D)                      │
│                                                           │
│  LAST NAME:  Hernandez                                    │
│  FIRST NAME: Carolina                                     │
│  ADDRESS:    875 Venice Ave.                              │
│  CITY: Los Angeles      STATE: CA   ZIP CODE: 90291       │
│  TELEPHONE: ( 310 ) 555-9876                              │
│  NATIVE            NATIVE                                  │
│  COUNTRY: Mexico   LANGUAGE: Spanish                      │
└─────────────────────────────────────────────────────────┘
```

1. What's her last name? Her last name is Hernandez. _____

2. What's her street? _____

3. What's her telephone number? _____

4. What's her area code? _____

5. What's her native language? _____

6. What country is she from? _____

Game Time

Divide the class into teams of eight or ten students.
Student 1 from each team: Stand up and say your name and native country.

> Student 1: My name is Carolina. I am from Mexico.

Student 2 from each team: Stand behind Student 1. Say his or her name and native country, and your name and native country.

> Student 2: Her name is Carolina. She is from Mexico. My name is Monica. I am from Brazil.

Student 3 from each team: Stand behind Students 1 and 2. Tell their names and native countries, and your name and native country.
Continue until the last student tells all the teammates' names and native countries.

Review

1 Read and Listen Read the story. Listen to the story.

My Classmates

Hello. I am Ping. My last name is Chang. I am from China. My English teacher is Alison Ryan. She is from New York. English is her native language. Carlos Garcia is one of my classmates. He is from El Salvador. Spanish is his native language. Marco and Carolina are from Mexico. Spanish is their native language, too. Han is from Vietnam, and Tanya is from Russia.

My classmates are from ten different countries. How many different countries are your classmates from?

2 Write Answer the questions.

1. What is Ping's last name? <u>Ping's last name is Chang.</u>

2. What is Alison's native language? _____

3. Where is Carlos from? _____

4. Where are Marco and Carolina from? _____

5. What is their native language? _____

6. How many countries are Ping's classmates from? _____

7. How many countries are your classmates from? _____

3 Listen Listen to the conversation. Write the missing information on the student registration form.

STUDENT REGISTRATION FORM

LAST NAME **Vidal**

FIRST NAME _____   MIDDLE INITIAL _____

ADDRESS _____ **Tree St.**   APT. _____

CITY **Santa Monica** _____

STATE **CA** _____   ZIP CODE **904** _____

TELEPHONE **(310)** _____

NATIVE COUNTRY **Colombia**   NATIVE LANGUAGE _____

4 Best Answer Bubble the correct answers.

	a	b	c	d

1. What's _____ first name? My first name is Monica.
   a) you   b) your   c) his   d) it   ○ ● ○ ○

2. _____ are from Colombia. Their native language is Spanish.
   a) He   b) We   c) It   d) They   ○ ○ ○ ○

3. The letter after D in the alphabet is _____ .
   a) A   b) E   c) I   d) F   ○ ○ ○ ○

4. The area code is _____ .
   a) 818   b) 90291   c) 555-1212   d) 25   ○ ○ ○ ○

5. He is from China. _____ native language is Chinese.
   a) My   b) Your   c) His   d) Her   ○ ○ ○ ○

6. Where is she from? _____ from Mexico.
   a) She   b) Is   c) She's   d) Her   ○ ○ ○ ○

5 **Match** Write the letter.

<u>h</u> **1.** A telephone number   **a.** Los Angeles

_____ **2.** A last name   **b.** Portuguese

_____ **3.** A city   **c.** 818

_____ **4.** A zip code   **d.** Monica

_____ **5.** A first name   **e.** Silva

_____ **6.** An address   **f.** 19033 Victory Blvd.

_____ **7.** A language   **g.** 91303

_____ **8.** An area code   **h.** 555-4163

6 **Write** Write the missing information from Activity 5.

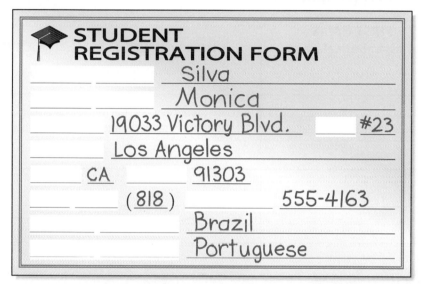

STUDENT REGISTRATION FORM

	Silva
	Monica
	19033 Victory Blvd. #23
	Los Angeles
CA	91303
(818)	555-4163
	Brazil
	Portuguese

7 **Write** Write about your class.

My classmates are from _____ different countries. One of my classmates is from _____. His name is _____. His native language is _____. One of my classmates is from _____. Her first name is _____. Her last name is _____. _____ of my classmates are from _____. Their native language is _____.

Write more sentences on a sheet of paper.

Word Help: Alphabetical order

Alphabetical order means to organize something by the alphabet.

These names are not in alphabetical order: Bob, Ping, Alison, Carlos.
Now, they are in alphabetical order: <u>A</u>lison, <u>B</u>ob, <u>C</u>arlos, <u>P</u>ing.

Write these names in alphabetical order:

Carlos _____

Monica _____

Angela _____

Tanya _____

8 **Teamwork Task** Work in teams of four or five. Complete the chart about your teammates.

FIRST NAME (in alphabetical order)	PHONE NUMBER	NATIVE COUNTRY

I can . . .			
• identify and write the letters of the alphabet.	1	2	3
• introduce myself.	1	2	3
• ask for and tell names.	1	2	3
• spell my name.	1	2	3
• identify and write numbers.	1	2	3
• ask for and tell addresses.	1	2	3
• ask for and tell phone numbers.	1	2	3
• ask for and tell native countries and languages.	1	2	3
• complete a registration form.	1	2	3
• identify and use the verb *be*.	1	2	3
• identify and use personal pronouns.	1	2	3
• identify and use possessive adjectives.	1	2	3

1 = not well   2 = OK   3 = very well

DOWNTOWN

9 **Write** Write the missing words in the story. Use these words: *am, is, are, My, Her, They, you, from, city, I'm.*

Alison: Good morning, class. I (1) _____ your new teacher. (2) _____ name is Alison Ryan.

Ping: My name is Ping Chang.
Alison: Nice to meet (3) _____ , Ping.

Ping: She (4) _____ my friend.
(5) _____ name is Jenny.
Alison: Hello, Jenny.

Ping: (6) _____ are my friends, too.
They (7) _____ from Mexico.

Alison: And where are you (8) _____ , Ping?
Ping: (9) _____ from China.

Jenny: Where are you from, Alison?
Alison: I'm from New York, but Los Angeles is my (10) _____ now. I love LA!

10 **Group Practice** Work in groups of three. Practice the story. Student 1 is Alison. Student 2 is Ping. Student 3 is Jenny.

School

GOALS

- ✓ Identify classroom objects.
- ✓ Describe a classroom.
- ✓ Identify school jobs.
- ✓ Understand titles (*Mr., Mrs., Ms., Miss*).
- ✓ Describe locations.
- ✓ Greet and introduce people.
- ✓ Respond to greetings.
- ✓ Follow classroom instructions.
- ✓ Address an envelope.
- ✓ Distinguish between singular and plural.
- ✓ Respond to *yes/no* questions with short answers.

1 **Listen** *Listen and repeat.*

1. a teacher
2. a student
3. a chalkboard
4. a piece of chalk
5. an eraser
6. a desk
7. a book
8. a pencil
9. a pen
10. a table
11. a chair
12. a notebook
13. a dictionary
14. a computer
15. a clock
16. a trash can
17. a bookcase

2 **Listen** *Listen and point to the words in the picture.*

3 **Pronunciation**

- teacher
- table
- student
- notebook
- chalkboard
- dictionary
- eraser
- computer
- pencil
- bookcase

1 **Say It** Listen to the conversations. Say them with a partner.

1. **A:** What's this?
   B: It's a pen.

2. **A:** What's that?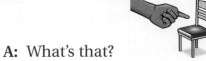
   B: It's a chair.

3. **A:** What's this?
   B: It's a _____ .

4. **A:** What's that?
   B: It's a _____ .

5. **A:** What's this?
   B: It's a _____ .

6. **A:** What's that?
   B: It's a _____ .

7. **A:** What's this?
   B: It's a _____ .

8. **A:** What's that?
   B: It's a _____ .

9. **A:** What's this?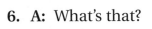
   B: It's a _____ .

10. **A:** What's that?
    B: It's a _____ .

2 **Pair Practice** Work with a partner. Point at things in the classroom on pages 22–23. Ask and answer questions.

Example: *Student 1:* What's that?
Student 2: It's a dictionary.

Word Help: Singular and plural

Singular means one. Plural means more than one.
Add an **-s** to most nouns to make them plural.

two books   one book

---

3 **Say It** Listen to the conversation. Say it with a partner.

A: What are they?
B: They are <u>books</u>.
A: How many <u>books</u>?
B: <u>Three</u> <u>books</u>.

Practice more conversations. Use the pictures below.

1.

2.

3.

4.

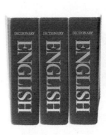

5.

6.

Yes/No questions and short answers

	Question	Affirmative	Negative
Singular	Is that a pencil?	Yes, it is.	No, it's not.
Plural	Are they books?	Yes, they are.	No, they're not.

Check Points:
✓ Use contractions with negative short answers.
✓ Don't use contractions with affirmative short answers.
Is that a book?   Yes, it is. (correct)   Yes, ~~it's~~. (not correct)

4 Say It Listen to the conversations. Say them with a partner.

A: Is that a <u>pencil</u>?
B: Yes, it is.

A: Is that a <u>pencil</u>?
B: No, it's not. It's a <u>pen</u>.

a pencil?

a pencil?

Practice more conversations. Use the pictures below.

1. a notebook?

2. a desk?

3. a computer?

4. a notebook?

5. a computer?

6. a chair?

5 **Say It** Listen to the conversations. Say them with a partner.

pencils?

A: Are they <u>pencils</u>?
B: Yes, they are.

A: Are they <u>pencils</u>?
B: No, they're not. They are <u>pens</u>.

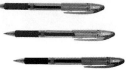

pencils?

Practice more conversations. Use the pictures below.

1. notebooks?

2. tables?

3. pieces of chalk?

6 **Listen** Listen. Circle the word you hear.

1. (pen)   pencil
2. textbook   notebook
3. desk   chair
4. chalkboard   chalk
5. clock   chalk
6. chair   teacher

7 **Teamwork Task** Work in teams of three or four. List things in your classroom. Write *a* or *an* if there is only one. Write a number if there is more than one.

Example: a teacher   25 books

Game Time

Your teacher will think of something in your classroom. Guess what it is.

Example: *Student 1:* Is it a pen?   *Teacher:* No, it isn't.
                 Student 2: Is it a pencil?   *Teacher:* Yes, it is.

1 **Say It** Listen to the conversation. Say it with a partner.

Ms. Ryan / teacher

A: Who is <u>she</u>?

B: That's <u>Ms. Ryan</u>.

A: Is <u>she</u> a student?

B: No, <u>she</u> isn't. <u>She's</u> a <u>teacher</u>.

A: Oh. My mistake!

Practice more conversations. Use the pictures below.

1. **Mr. Bell / counselor**

2. **Miss Ramirez /
teacher's assistant**

3. **Ms. Castillo / security guard**

Word Help: Titles

Use titles with last names.   John Smith = Mr. Smith
Do not use titles with first names.   John Smith = ~~Mr. John~~ (not correct)

Title	Pronunciation	Meaning
Mr.	/ mister /	a man, married or single
Ms.	/ miz /	a woman, married or single
Miss	/ miss /	a single woman
Mrs.	/ missiz /	a married woman

2 Pronunciation Listen and repeat the titles.

1. Mr.   /mister/ Jones
2. Ms.   /miz/ Jones
3. Miss   /miss/ Jones
4. Mrs.   /missiz/ Jones

3 Write Complete the short answers.

Question	Affirmative	Negative
1. Are you a student?	Yes, I _____ .	No, I'm not.
2. Is he a student?	Yes, he _____ .	No, he isn't.
3. Is she a student?	Yes, she is.	No, she _____ .
4. Are we students?	Yes, we _____ .	No, we aren't.
5. Are they students?	Yes, they are.	No, they _____ .

4 Say It Listen to the conversation. Say it with a partner.

Ms. Ryan

A: Is <u>Ms. Ryan</u> in the classroom?
B: No, <u>she</u> isn't.
A: Where is <u>she</u>?
B: <u>She's</u> in the <u>office</u>.

Practice more conversations. Use the pictures below.

1. Ping

2. Marco

3. Monica

⑤ Write Write the short answers. Use contractions for negative answers.

1. Is Carlos a counselor?   No, __he__ __isn't__.
2. Are Ping and Monica teachers?   No, _____ _____.
3. Is Tanya a student?   Yes, _____ _____.
4. Are you a student?   Yes, _____ _____.
5. Are they pencils?   Yes, _____ _____.
6. Are you in the cafeteria?   No, _____ _____.

Word Help: Prepositions of location

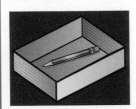      

in the box   on the box   under the box

⑥ Say It Listen to the conversation. Say it with a partner.

on the desk?

A: Is the dictionary <u>on the desk</u>?
B: No, it isn't.
A: Where is it?
B: It's <u>in the trash can</u>.
A: Please put it <u>on the desk</u>.
B: OK.

1. on the table?   2. on the bookcase?   3. on your desk?

Word Help: Prepositions of location

next to

between

in front of

in back of / behind

7 **Write** Write two sentences about each picture.

1. The pen is on the desk.

   The pen is between the erasers.

2. _____

   _____

3. _____

   _____

4. _____

   _____

8 **Listen** Listen and write the names of the students in the correct places.

Front

Monica		

Back

9 **Pair Practice** Work with a partner. Ask and answer questions about the students.

Example: *Student 1:* Where is Monica?
Student 2: Monica is in front of . . .

10 **Teamwork Task** Work in teams of three or four. Write sentences about your classmates. Use *next to, between, in front of,* and *behind.*

1. _____ is next to _____ .
2. _____ is in front of _____ .
3. _____ is behind _____ .
4. _____ is between _____ and _____ .

Write more sentences on a sheet of paper.

Game Time

Your teacher will think of the name of a student. Ask yes/no questions to guess who the student is.

Example: *Student:* Is it a she?
Teacher: Yes, it is.
Student: Is she behind Maria?

If the teacher says "No," another student asks a question.

This is Mr. Bell.

1 **Say It** Listen to the conversation. Say it with two partners.

A: This is <u>Mr. Bell. He is a counselor</u>.
B: Hello, <u>Mr. Bell</u>. How are you today?
C: I'm fine, thank you. How are you?
B: I'm <u>very good</u>.

very good

Practice more conversations. Use the pictures below.

1. OK   2. not bad   3. great

Word Help: How are you?

great   very good   fine/OK/not bad   so-so   terrible

2 **Group Practice** Find a partner. Introduce your partner to other classmates.

Example: *Student 1:* Hello. This is _____ . He/She is a student.
Student 2: Hello. How are you today?
Student 3: I'm _____ . How are you?
Student 2: I'm _____ .
Student 3: OK. See you later.
Student 2: Bye.

Say It Listen to the conversation. Say it with a partner.

A: Please <u>write your name</u>.
B: <u>Write my name</u>?
A: Yes. <u>Write your name</u> in your notebook.
B: OK.

**write your name /
in your notebook**

Practice more conversations. Use the pictures below.

1. **sign your name / on the form**

2. **open your book / to page 22**

3. **circle the answer / in your book**

4. **write the answer / on the board**

5. **raise your hand / if you know the answer**

6. **sit down / behind Ping**

1. _____   2. _____

_____   _____

_____   _____

X_____   _____

5 **Read** Read the sentences. Check your answers above.
1. Write your first name next to number one.
2. Write these letters next to number 2: A, E, I, O, and U.
3. Write number 9 under letter A.
4. Write number 5 under letter I.
5. Write number 3 between number 9 and number 5.
6. Circle the letter E.
7. Underline the letter U.
8. Write your address under your name.
9. Sign your name next to the letter X.
10. Write your zip code between your address and your signature.
11. Write your classroom number next to your zip code.
12. Write your teacher's name under your classroom number.
13. Raise your hand if you have no mistakes.

Word Help: Address an envelope

Alison Ryan
6200 Apple Ave.
Woodland Hills, CA 91367

Sender's Address

Mr. Don Mathews
3225 Melrose St.
Hollywood, CA 90019

Recipient's Address

U.S. POSTAGE

6 Pair Practice
Work with a partner. Student 1: Read the sentences.
Student 2: Listen and write on the envelope.

1. Write your last name next to number one.
2. Write your first name next to number two.
3. Write your address next to number three.
4. Write your city, state, and zip code under your address.
5. Write your teacher's title (Mr., Ms., Mrs., or Miss) next to number five.
6. Write your teacher's first and last name next to number six.
7. Write the name of your school next to number seven.
8. Write the school address next to number eight.
9. Write the city your school is in next to number nine.
10. Write your state and zip code next to number ten.

1. _____ 2. _____

3. _____

4. _____

5. _____ 6. _____

7. _____

8. _____

9. _____ 10. _____

Now, Student 2: Read the sentences. Student 1: Write on the envelope.

7 Teamwork Task
Work in teams of three.
Student 1 is the writer.
Student 2 is the sender.
Student 3 is the recipient.

Student 1: Draw an envelope. Ask Student 2 and Student 3 for their names and addresses. Write them in the correct place on the envelope.

1 Read and Listen Read the story. Listen to the story.

My Classroom

Hello again. This is Ping. I am in my English class right now. Ten other students are in my classroom, too. My friend Monica is next to me. Tanya is behind her, and Marco is behind Tanya. Ms. Ryan, my teacher, is in front of the class. The door is open. Mr. Bell, the counselor, is next to the door. "Good morning, Ms. Ryan," he says. "How are you?"

My name is Ms. Ryan. This class is ESL 1.

"I'm fine," she says. "How are you?"

The chalkboard is behind Ms. Ryan. Her name is on the chalkboard. The name of our class, ESL 1, is under her name. There is a piece of chalk in Ms. Ryan's hand. Two pens and ten pencils are on her desk. An English book is on her desk, too. "Please open your books," Ms. Ryan says. The name of my book is *Downtown*. I think it's a great book!

2 Write Answer the questions.

1. Where is Ping right now?   <u>Ping is in her English class.</u>

2. How many students are in the class? _____

3. Is Monica next to Ping? _____

4. Is Marco next to Ping? _____

5. Is Tanya between Monica and Marco? _____

6. How is Ms. Ryan today? _____

7. What is on the chalkboard? _____

8. How many pencils are on the teacher's desk? _____

3 Write Write the things you see in the classroom.

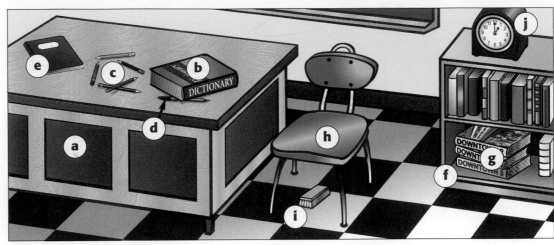

a. _____ f. _____

b. _____ g. _____

c. _____ h. _____

d. _____ i. _____

e. _____ j. _____

4 Write Write sentences about the picture. Use prepositions of location.

Example: *The dictionary is on the desk.*

5 Pair Practice Work with a partner. Ask and answer questions about the classroom on this page and the classroom on pages 22–23.

Example: *Student 1:* Where is the clock in this classroom?
Student 2: It's on the bookcase.
Student 2: Where is the clock in that classroom?
Student 1: It's on the wall.

_____

_____

_____

_____

_____

_____

_____

6 **Best Answer** Bubble the correct answers.

	a	b	c	d

1. What's that? _____ a pen.   ○ ○ ● ○
   a. That   **b.** Is
   c. It's   **d.** It

2. Where are the books? _____ on the table.   ○ ○ ○ ○
   a. They   **b.** They're
   c. It's   **d.** It

3. Who is that? That's _____ . He's a teacher.   ○ ○ ○ ○
   a. Ms. Ryan   **b.** Miss Bhatt
   c. Mr. Edwards   **d.** Miss Jones

4. How are you today?   ○ ○ ○ ○
   a. Not bad.   **b.** I am.
   c. Thank you.   **d.** And you?

5. Is Ms. Ryan in the classroom? No, she _____ .   ○ ○ ○ ○
   a. not   **b.** don't
   c. isn't   **d.** is

7 **Listen** Listen and write in the box below.

1. _____   _____   2. _____

   _____   _____   _____

3. _____   _____   _____

8 **Pronunciation** Listen and repeat the words. Stress the correct syllables.

teacher   notebook   dictionary   computer   classroom   between

Now, listen and underline the stressed syllable in these words.

eraser   pencil   table   bookcase   behind   student

Say the words again.

9 Teamwork Task Work in teams of three or four. Write about your classroom. Use names and numbers and prepositions of location. Write as many sentences as you can.

Example: <u>Twenty-five books are in the bookcase.</u>

_____

_____

_____

_____

_____

_____

_____

_____

_____

_____

I can . . .			
• identify classroom objects.	1	2	3
• describe a classroom.	1	2	3
• identify school jobs.	1	2	3
• understand titles (Mr., Mrs., Ms., Miss).	1	2	3
• describe locations.	1	2	3
• greet and introduce people.	1	2	3
• respond to greetings.	1	2	3
• follow classroom instructions.	1	2	3
• address an envelope.	1	2	3
• distinguish between singular and plural.	1	2	3
• respond to yes/no questions with short answers.	1	2	3

1 = not well   2 = OK   3 = very well

Ping: Good morning, (1) _____ Ryan. How (2) _____ you today?

Ms. Ryan: I'm (3) _____ , Ping. How are you?
Ping: Fine, (4) _____ .

Ms. Ryan: Please (5) _____ down and (6) _____ your books.

Ms. Ryan: Jenny, go to the chalkboard. Pick up a (7) _____ . It's (8) _____ the eraser.

Ms. Ryan: Write your name (9) _____ the board.
Jenny: Where?
Ms. Ryan: (10) _____ my name.

Ms. Ryan: OK, class. What's her name?
Class: Her name is Jenny.
Ms. Ryan: Great! Don't forget it.

Group Practice Work in groups of four. Practice the story. Student 1 is Ms. Ryan, Student 2 is Ping, Student 3 is Jenny, and Student 4 is the "class".

GOALS

- ✓ Ask for and tell time.
- ✓ Write the time.
- ✓ Ask about and describe the weather.
- ✓ Use Fahrenheit to tell temperature.
- ✓ Read, write, and say the days of the week.
- ✓ Read a class schedule.
- ✓ Read an appointment card.
- ✓ Read, write, and say the months of the year.
- ✓ Ask for and tell birthdays.
- ✓ Read a calendar.
- ✓ Write dates.
- ✓ Identify holidays.
- ✓ Read business schedules.

Sunday	Monday ③	Tuesday
4	5	6
	PARTY AT JENNY'S ⟨8:00 P.M.⟩ ⑥	

January ①

2009

² 2009

Thursday

Friday

Saturday

sday

1

2

3 ⁴

5
New Year's Day

8 ⁷

9

10

Dr. GRAY
2:30 P.M.

4

15

16

17

1 Listen *Listen and repeat.*

1. a month
2. a year
3. a day
4. a date
5. a holiday
6. a time
7. an appointment

2 Listen *Listen to the words. Look at the picture. Repeat.*

3 Pronunciation

●
holiday

●
appointment

What time is it?

Word Help: Time

7:00 = seven o'clock   7:05 = seven-oh-five   7:10 = seven-ten

Write the times below.

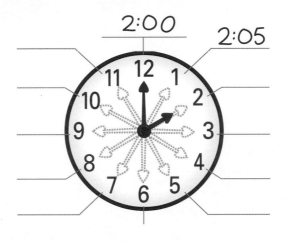

2:00

2:05

1 Say It Listen to the conversation. Say it with a partner.

3:15

A: What time is it?

B: It's <u>three o'clock</u>.

A: What time is your appointment?

B: <u>Three-fifteen</u>.

A: That's good. You're on time.

Practice more conversations. Use the pictures below.

1. 5:45

2. 4:30

3. 8:00

Say It Listen to the conversation. Say it with a partner.

one o'clock

A: What time is it?

B: It's <u>a quarter after one</u>.

A: I'm sorry. What time is it?

B: It's <u>one-fifteen</u>.

A: What time is your appointment?

B: <u>One o'clock</u>.

A: That's bad. You're late!

Practice more conversations. Use the pictures below.

1. 1:15

2. 3:30

3. 4:45

Culture Tip

Business time

Always arrive before the time of your business appointment. For appointments, arriving five minutes late is very late.

3 Listen Listen and write the times. Then draw the hands on the clocks.

1. 6:45

   six forty-five

2. _____

   _____

3. _____

   _____

4. _____

   _____

5. _____

   _____

6. _____

   _____

4 Write Write the times. Use *before*, *to*, *past*, or *after*.

1. 5:20   twenty after five _____

2. 12:05   _____

3. 10:15   _____

4. 11:55   _____

5. 9:45   _____

6. 3:10   _____

Word Help: Temperature (Fahrenheit scale)

Write the words next to the thermometer.

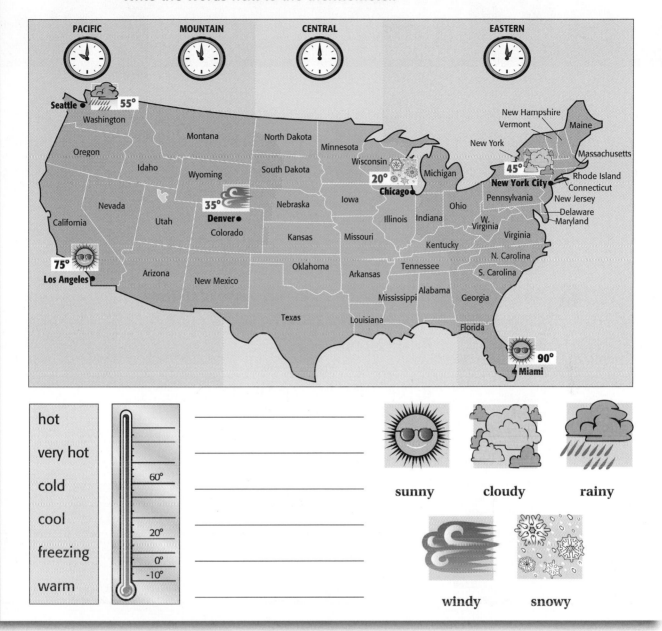

hot	
very hot	
cold	
cool	
freezing	
warm	

sunny　　cloudy　　rainy

windy　　snowy

⑤ Pair Practice Work with a partner. Ask and answer questions about the time and weather.

Example: *Student 1:* What time is it in Miami?
Student 2: It's one o'clock in the afternoon.
Student 1: How is the weather in Miami?
Student 2: It's sunny and hot.
Student 1: What's the temperature?
Student 2: It's 90 degrees.

⑥ Group Practice Draw a clock. Make it any time you like. Then ask your classmates what time it is on their clocks.

What day is today?

1 **Listen** Listen and repeat the days of the week.

the weekend	weekdays					the weekend
Sunday SUN	Monday MON	Tuesday TUES	Wednesday WED	Thursday THURS	Friday FRI	Saturday SAT

2 **Say It** Listen to the conversation. Say it with a partner.

A: What day is today?

B: It's Monday.

A: Monday? Are you sure?

B: Yes, I am. Today is Monday and tomorrow is Tuesday.

Practice more conversations. Use the pictures below.

1.   2.   3.

Note: Capitalize the first letter of the days of the week.
Monday (correct)   ~~monday~~ (not correct)

3 **Write** Complete the sentences with a day of the week.

1. The day after Monday is _____ .

2. The day after Thursday is _____ .

3. The day after Saturday is _____ .

4. The day before Thursday is _____ .

5. The day before Wednesday is _____ .

4 **Say It** Listen to the conversation. Say it with a partner.

ENGLISH CLASS
Mon. & Wed.
8:00–11:00 AM

A: When is your class?
B: <u>On Monday and Wednesday</u>.
A: What time?
B: <u>Eight o'clock</u>.
A: How long is it?
B: It's three hours—from <u>eight o'clock</u> to <u>eleven o'clock</u>.

Practice more conversations. Use the pictures below.

Reading Class
Mon.–Fri.
1:00–4:00 PM

1.

ESL CLASS
Tues. & Thurs.
6:30–9:30 PM

2.

Conversation Class
Mon., Wed. & Fri.
10:00–1:00 PM

3.

Word Help: _from, to_
Use _from_ to tell when something starts. Use _to_ to tell when it ends.
   6:00–6:30 means **from** six o'clock **to** six-thirty.
   Monday–Friday means **from** Monday **to** Friday.

5 **Group Practice** Pretend you have an appointment this week. Write the day and time. Then ask your classmates the day and time of their appointments.

Example: *Student 1:* When is your appointment?
   Student 2: It's on Monday.
   Student 1: What time?
   Student 2: It's at 6:30.

6 **Listen** Listen and write the days and times.

1.

2.

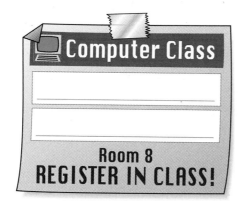

3.

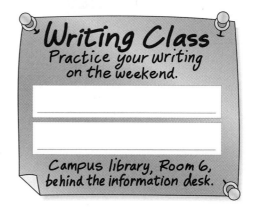

4.

7 **Pair Practice** Work with a partner. Ask and answer questions about the classes. Ask about days, times, and locations.

Example: *Student 1:* When is the ESL 2 class?

              Student 2: It's on Saturday.

              Student 1: What time?

              Student 2: It's from nine in the morning to one
                          in the afternoon.

              Student 1: What room is it in?

              Student 2: It's in Room 34.

8 Pair Practice Work with a partner. Ask and answer questions about the appointments.

Example: Dr. Gray—8:00 AM

A: When is your appointment with <u>Doctor Gray</u>?

B: It's at <u>8:00 AM</u>.

A: <u>Eight o'clock in the morning</u>?

B: Yes, that's right.

1. the dentist—4:30 PM
2. the counselor—9:45 AM
3. Ms. Ryan—7:00 PM
4. Professor McBride—12:30 PM
5. Mrs. West—10:00 PM

9 Teamwork Task Work in teams of three or four. Ask your teammates to tell you about an appointment they have. Complete the chart

NAME	DAY OF APPOINTMENT	TIME	PART OF THE DAY
Ping Chang	Tuesday	10:30	morning

Game Time

Your teacher will secretly write the day and time of an appointment. Ask yes/no questions to find out when it is.

Example: *Student 1:* Is it on Monday? *Teacher:* No, it isn't.

Student 2: Is it on Friday? *Teacher:* Yes, it is.

The Calendar

1 **Listen** Listen and repeat the months of the year.

January	February	March	April	May	June
July	August	September	October	November	December

> **Note: Seasons**
> Spring = March 20 – June 20   Summer = June 21 – September 21
> Fall = September 22 – December 20   Winter = December 21 – March19

2 **Say It** Listen to the conversation. Say it with a partner.

April first

A: When is <u>Ping's</u> birthday?
B: It's in <u>April</u>.
A: What's the date?
B: It's on <u>April first</u>.

Practice more conversations. Use the pictures below.

1. September second

2. July third

3. November fourth

> **Note: Use 's for possessive**
> Ping's birthday = the birthday of Ping

3 **Write** Complete the sentences with months of the year

1. The month after February is _____.
2. The month after July is _____.
3. The month before June is _____.
4. The month before May is _____.
5. The month after October is _____.
6. The month after December is _____.

4 **Listen** Listen and repeat the ordinal numbers.

SUNDAY	MONDAY	TUESDAY	WEDNESDAY	THURSDAY	FRIDAY	SATURDAY
	1 (First)	**2** (Second)	**3** (Third)	**4** (Fourth)	**5** (Fifth)	**6** (Sixth)
7 (Seventh)	**8** (Eighth)	**9** (Ninth)	**10** (Tenth)	**11** (Eleventh)	**12** (Twelfth)	**13** (Thirteenth)
14 (Fourteenth)	**15** (Fifteenth)	**16** (Sixteenth)	**17** (Seventeenth)	**18** (Eighteenth)	**19** (Nineteenth)	**20** (Twentieth)
21 (Twenty-first)	**22** (Twenty-second)	**23** (Twenty-third)	**24** (Twenty-fourth)	**25** (Twenty-fifth)	**26** (Twenty-sixth)	**27** (Twenty-seventh)
28 (Twenty-eighth)	**29** (Twenty-ninth)	**30** (Thirtieth)	**31** (Thirty-first)			

January

5 **Pronunciation** Listen and repeat the words with a /th/ sound.

three   third   Thursday   fourth   fifth   sixth   thirteen   thirty

Word Help: Days and dates
Use *day* for a day of the week: Monday, Tuesday, etc.
Use *date* for a month and a day: January 4th, May 5th, etc.

6 **Listen** Listen and write the dates you hear.

1. _August 2nd_ _____
2. _____
3. _____
4. _____
5. _____

6. _____
7. _____
8. _____
9. _____
10. _____

7 **Pair Practice** Work with a partner. Point to a date on the calendar. Your partner will say the date.

Example: *Student 1:* What's this date?
Student 2: That's January first.

8 **Say It** Listen to the conversation. Say it with a partner.

A: What is <u>Ping's</u> date of birth?

B: <u>Her</u> birthday is on <u>April first</u>.

A: What year was <u>she</u> born?

B: <u>She</u> was born in 1982. So, <u>her</u> date of birth is <u>April first</u>, <u>nineteen eighty-two</u>.

Practice more conversations. Use the pictures below.

1.

2.

Note: Month, day, year
In the U.S., give dates in this order: month, day, year.
July 4, 2009 = 7/4/09
Number the months in order from 1 to 12.

_____ January	_____ March	_____ September
_____ August	_____ July	_____ February
_____ May	_____ December	_____ November
_____ April	_____ October	_____ June

9 **Write** Write the dates.

1. August 9, 1995   <u>*8/9/95*</u>   6. 6/5/65 _____

2. January 5, 2005 _____ 7. 2/12/07 _____

3. March 8, 2007 _____ 8. 4/29/60 _____

4. September 22, 1969 _____ 9. 10/6/73 _____

5. November 11, 2001 _____ 10. 12/25/06 _____

10 **Say It** Listen to the conversation. Say it with a partner.

Independence Day

A: Independence Day is a holiday in the United States.
B: When is Independence Day?
A: It's in July.
B: What day in July?
A: It's on July fourth.

Practice more conversations. Use the pictures below.

1. New Year's Day

2. Valentine's Day

3. Halloween

11 **Listen** Listen and write the dates of the holidays.

1. Labor Day _____
2. Thanksgiving _____
3. Presidents' Day _____
4. Memorial Day _____
5. Christmas Day _____

GRAMMAR CHECK

Prepositions for time

Use *in* for a month, a year, a part of the day, and a season of the year.
  in August   **in** 2010   **in** the morning   **in** winter
Use *on* for a day or a date.
  on Monday   **on** September 26th
Use *at* for a time and with *night*, *noon*, and *midnight*.
  at 8 AM   **at** noon

12 **Write** Write the correct preposition. Use *from, to, in, on,* or *at*.

1. ABC Bakery opens _____ six o'clock _____ Saturday.

2. Student Bookstore is open weekdays _____ 7:00 AM _____ 3:00 PM.

3. ABC Bakery is closed _____ Sunday.

4. Student Bookstore closes for vacation _____ July.

5. Student Bookstore closes _____ 12:00 PM _____ Saturday.

6. ABC Bakery opens _____ seven o'clock _____ the morning _____ weekdays.

13 **Teamwork Task** Work with a group of seven to ten students. Ask your teammates their birthdays. Then line up by order of birthdays. The person with the birthday closest to January 1 is first in line.

Game Time

Ask *yes/no* questions to guess your teacher's birthday. If the answer is yes, ask another question.

Example: *Student 1:* Is your birthday in May?   *Teacher:* No, it isn't.

  Student 2: Is your birthday in April?   *Teacher:* Yes, it is.

  Student 2: Is your birthday April 3rd?   *Teacher:* Yes, it is.

1 **Read and Listen** Read and listen to the story. Underline the dates.

Birthdays

All of Ping's friends in her English class have birthdays in different months. Julia's birthday is on January first, New Year's Day. Tanya's birthday is in February, on the fourteenth. That's Valentine's Day. Han Do's birthday is on March fifteenth. And, of course, Ping's birthday is in April, on the first. Her date of birth is 4/1/82.

Carlos has a birthday in the spring, on May 5th. That's a holiday in Mexico. Jenny's birthday is on the first day of summer, June 21. And Marco's birthday is on 7/3, the day before Independence Day. The fourth of July is a big holiday in the United States. It's the birthday of the country. The U.S. is more than 200 years old. Monica's birthday is in September, on the second. She isn't 200 years old. She's only 29.

Today is October 6th. It is a Thursday and it is a special day for Ms. Ryan because today is her birthday. Right now it is 11:00 and that's a good time for a birthday party for Ms. Ryan's special day. So . . .

"Happy birthday to you,
Happy birthday to you,
Happy birthday, Ms. Ryan,
Happy birthday to you!"

2 **Write** Write the dates in the story with words and numbers. Then write something about each date.

January 1	1/1	Julia's birthday, New Year's Day
_____	_____	_____
_____	_____	_____
_____	_____	_____
_____	_____	_____
_____	_____	_____
_____	_____	_____
_____	_____	_____
_____	_____	_____

③ Match Look at the calendar. Write the letters.

_____ 1. January 9, 2009   **a.** a year

_____ 2. 2009   **b.** Sunday

_____ 3. Thursday   **c.** the third

_____ 4. the day after Saturday   **d.** a holiday

_____ 5. January 1st   **e.** a date

_____ 6. the day before January 4th   **f.** a day of the week

④ Write Use the calendar to answer the questions.

1. What day of the week is New Year's Day?

_____

2. When is the appointment with Dr. Ona?

_____

3. When is John's birthday?

_____

4. What time is Ping's English class?

_____

5. What days does Ping go to English class?

_____

5 Best Answer Bubble the correct answers.

a b c

1. Three-fifteen is the same as _____ .
   a) a quarter after three   b) a quarter to three
   c) half past three

   ○ ○ ○

2. October 14th is a _____ .
   a) month   b) day   c) date

   ○ ○ ○

3. My appointment is _____ Friday.
   a) on   b) at   c) in

   ○ ○ ○

4. My class starts at 7:00 _____ the morning.
   a) on   b) at   c) in

   ○ ○ ○

5. My English class is from 7:00 PM _____ 10:00 PM.
   a) to   b) at   c) after

   ○ ○ ○

6. New Year's Day is on January _____ .
   a) month   b) first   c) day

   ○ ○ ○

6 Listen Listen and write the days, dates, and times.

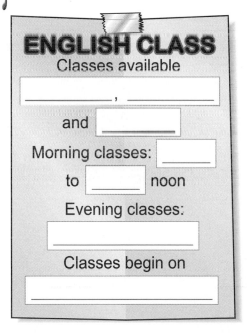

ENGLISH CLASS
Classes available

_____ , _____

and _____

Morning classes: _____
to _____ noon

Evening classes:
_____

Classes begin on
_____

1.

ESL Conversation Class

Available from

_____ to _____

Mornings from

_____ to _____

Starts

_____

2.

7 Teamwork Task Work in teams of five or six. Ask your teammates their birthdays. Write their birthdays in order by month. Then write sentences about your team.

BIRTHDAYS		
ORDER	**DATE**	**STUDENT NAME**
First		
Second		

Example: José is first in our group. His birthday is January 22nd.

_____

_____

_____

_____

_____

_____

I can . . .			
• identify classroom objects.	1	2	3
• ask for and tell time.	1	2	3
• write the time.	1	2	3
• ask about and describe the weather.	1	2	3
• use Fahrenheit to tell temperature.	1	2	3
• read, write, and say the days of the week.	1	2	3
• read a class schedule.	1	2	3
• read an appointment card.	1	2	3
• read, write, and say the months of the year.	1	2	3
• ask for and tell birthdays.	1	2	3
• read a calendar.	1	2	3
• write dates.	1	2	3
• identify common holidays.	1	2	3
• read business schedules.	1	2	3

1 = not well   2 = OK   3 = very well

8 **Write** Write the missing words in the story. Use these words: *day, date, month, Monday, October, holiday, sixth, birthday, calendar.*

Jenny: What (1) _____ is today, Ms. Ryan?

Alison: Today is (2) _____ .
Jenny: What (3) _____ is it now?

Ping: It's (4) _____ right now, Jenny.
Jenny: And what is the (5) _____ in October?
Ping: The (6) _____ says that Monday is October (7) _____ .

Jenny: And what is special about October 6th?
Is it a (8) _____ ?
Ping: No, it isn't a holiday.

Monica: But it is a special day because today is our teacher's (9) _____ .

Jenny, Monica, Ping: Happy Birthday, Ms. Ryan, Happy birthday to you!

9 **Group Practice** Work in groups of four. Practice the story. Student 1 is Jenny. Student 2 is Alison. Student 3 is Ping. Student 4 is Monica.

Shopping

① Listen *Listen and repeat.*

1. a jacket
2. a blouse
3. pants
4. shoes
5. a suit
6. a sweater
7. jeans
8. boots
9. a dress
10. a belt
11. shorts
12. a T-shirt
13. sneakers

② Pronunciation

•
jacket
•
sweater
•
sneakers

63

1 **Say It** Listen to the conversation. Say it with a partner.

A: How much is this?

B: It's <u>ten</u> dollars.

A: Are you sure?

B: Yes, I'm positive. It's a <u>ten</u>-dollar bill.

Practice more conversations. Use the pictures below.

1.　　　　　　　　　　2.　　　　　　　　　　3.

Word Help: Coins

a penny, | **a nickel,** | **a dime,** | **a quarter,** | **a half dollar,**
one cent | **five cents** | **ten cents** | **twenty-five cents** | **fifty cents**

---

2 **Write** Write the amounts of money.

1. _____ $21.00 _____

_____ twenty-one dollars _____

2. _____

_____

3. _____

_____

4. _____

_____

3 **Say It** Listen to the conversation. Say it with a partner.

A: How much are the <u>T-shirts</u>?

B: They're <u>ten dollars and fifty cents</u>.

A: How much do you have?

B: I have <u>twenty dollars</u>.

A: Great.

Practice more conversations. Use the pictures below.

1.

2.

3.

Culture Tip

Credit cards and debit cards

A credit card is like a loan. You pay back the money you use with *interest*. You don't pay interest when you use a debit card. You use your own money.

have/has	
Subject	**Verb**
I	have
you	have
he/she/it	has
we	have
you	have
they	have

4 **Write** Complete the sentences with *have* or *has*. Write the amounts.

1. ($20) How much money does Jenny have?

   <u>She has twenty dollars.</u>

2. ($10.75) How much money does Marco have in his pocket?

   He _____ _____ dollars and _____ cents.

3. ($35) How much money do Lucy and Ricky have?

   They _____ _____ dollars.

4. ($88) How much money does Tanya have?

   She _____ _____ dollars.

5. ($.90) How much cash does Carlos have?

   He _____ _____ cents.

6. ($?) How much cash do you have in your pocket?

   I _____ _____ .

5 **Group Practice** Ask five or six students how many quarters they have in their pockets. Remember what they tell you. Tell your teacher how many quarters each person has.

Example: *Student 1:* How many quarters do you have in your pocket?
         Student 2: I have three quarters.

6 **Listen** Listen and write the money in the boxes.

1. ALISON	2. MARCO AND JENNY	3. PING	4. HAN
$20 bill $5 bill two $1 bills			

7 **Write** Write a sentence about each box above. Use *have* or *has* and the total amount of money.

1. Alison has twenty-seven dollars. _____

2. _____

3. _____

4. _____

8 **Teamwork Task** Work in teams of four or five. Ask your teammates how much change they have in their pockets (coins only). Complete the chart.

NAME	AMOUNT OF CHANGE

Now, write sentences about your teammates.

Game Time

Everyone in the class drops one coin (a penny, a nickel, a dime, etc.) into the teacher's piggy bank (or cup). If you don't have a coin, drop in a piece of paper with the name of a coin. Each student guesses how much is in the bank. The student who guesses closest to the correct amount wins!

Clothes and Colors

Word Help: Colors

| red | orange | yellow | green | blue | purple | pink | brown | white | black |

1 Listen Listen and repeat the colors. Then point at something in your classroom for each color.

2 Write Look at pages 62–63. Write the color next to the clothing you see.

green jacket   _____ boots   _____ sweater

_____ blouse   _____ shorts   _____ belt

_____ shoes   _____ T-shirt   _____ jeans

_____ dress   _____ suit   _____ sneakers

3 Write Which clothing words are singular? Which are plural? Write the words from Activity 2.

SINGULAR	PLURAL

Note: *is/are*

Use *is* for singular nouns.   The jacket **is** green.
Use *are* for plural nouns.   The boots **are** black.

4 Pair Practice Work with a partner. Ask and answer questions about the clothes and the colors on pages 62–63.

Example: *Student 1:* What color is the jacket?
              Student 2: It's green.
              Student 1: What color are the boots?
              Student 2: They are black.

5 **Say It** Listen to the conversation. Say it with a partner.

A: I need a new pair of <u>shorts</u>.

B: What color <u>shorts</u> do you want?

A: I like <u>red</u>.

B: Here's a pair of <u>red</u> <u>shorts</u>.

A: Thanks.

Practice more conversations. Use the pictures below.

1.

2.

3.

> **Note: Word order**
> Say the color before the noun.
> black shorts (correct)
> ~~shorts black~~ (not correct)

6 **Group Practice** Work with a large group or the whole class. Walk around the room. Ask your classmates, "What's your favorite color?" Write a classmate's name next to each color.

blue _____   red _____

green _____   pink _____

white _____   black _____

brown _____   other _____

Simple present	
Subject	*Verb*
I/you/we/they	like
	want
	need
he/she/it	likes
	wants
	needs

7 **Say It** Listen to the conversation. Say it with a partner.

Jenny / leather jacket

A: <u>Jenny</u> wants a new <u>leather jacket</u>.

B: What color does she want?

A: She wants <u>black or brown</u>.

B: What size does she need?

A: She needs a <u>small</u>.

Practice more conversations. Use the pictures below.

1. **Carlos / shirt**

2. **Tanya / dress**

Word Help: Sizes

| small | medium | large | extra large |

Tanya's Closet   **Jenny's Closet**

8 **Write** What kind of clothes do Tanya and Jenny like? List the things you see in their closets. Write complete sentences.

1. <u>Tanya likes brown shoes.</u>

2. _____

3. _____

4. _____

5. _____

6. _____

7. _____

8. _____

9. _____

10. _____

9 Write Write the correct form of the verb.

1. (like) Ping _____ black jackets.
2. (need) I _____ a new jacket.
3. (want) Marco and Carlos _____ new shoes.
4. (like) We _____ blue sweaters.
5. (want) Do you _____ a suit?
6. (need) Tanya _____ a new bathing suit.
7. (like) Tanya and I _____ black jackets.
8. (want) Jenny _____ a new pair of shoes.
9. (have) Ping _____ a new jacket.
10. (need) I _____ new clothes.

10 Teamwork Task Work in teams of four. Ask your teammates what color shoes, pants, shirts, and jackets they like to wear. Complete the chart.

NAME	SHOES	PANTS	SHIRTS	JACKETS

Now, work together to write sentences about your team. Write as many sentences as you can.

Examples: José likes brown shoes.
Rosa and Carmen like black shoes.

Game Time

Student 1: Stand up and say something you like to wear. ("I like to wear white shirts.")
Student 2: Stand up and say what your classmate likes to wear and what you like to wear. ("He likes to wear white shirts, and I like to wear blue jeans.")
Keep adding students until someone makes a mistake. The last student before the mistake wins!

May I help you?

① Say It Listen to the conversation. Say it with a partner.

A: May I help you?

B: Yes, please. I'm looking for a <u>black leather jacket</u>.

A: Here's a <u>black leather jacket</u>. What size do you need?

B: I need a <u>medium</u>, I think.

A: This is a <u>medium</u>.

B: How much is it?

A: This one is <u>$149</u>.

B: Oh, that's a lot.

Practice more conversations. Use the pictures below.

1.

2.

3.

Culture Tip

Sizes

Sizes are different for different kinds of clothes.

Women's pants and dresses use numbers—for example, size 6 or size 8.

Sometimes pants use inches—for example, 30-inch waist by 32-inch length.

Men's suit jackets have a number and a letter—for example, 40R = size 40 regular.

Simple present negative		
Subject	**Negative**	**Verb**
I/you/we/they	do not (don't)	like want need
he/she/it	does not (doesn't)	like want need

2 **Say It** Listen to the conversation. Say it with a partner.

shoes

A: Do you like <u>red</u> <u>shoes</u>?

B: No, I don't.

A: What color <u>shoes</u> do you like?

B: I like <u>black</u> or <u>brown</u> <u>shoes</u>. I definitely don't like <u>red</u> <u>shoes</u>!

Practice more conversations. Use the pictures below.

1. T-shirts

2. belts

3. shorts

4. pants

5. suits

6. shoes

3 **Write** What color clothes does your partner like? Write sentences.

Example: He likes black shoes. He likes white T-shirts.

GRAMMAR CHECK

Questions with *do, does*		
Do/Does	*Subject*	*Verb*
Do	I you we they	like	black jackets?
Does	he she it	like	black jackets?

Check Points:
  ✓ Use *do* with the pronouns *I, you, we,* and *they.*
  Do you like leather jackets?   Yes, **I do.**
  ✓ Use *does* with the pronouns *he, she,* and *it.*
  Does Jenny like leather jackets?   Yes, **she does.**

4 **Write** Complete the sentences with *do* or *does.*

1. _____ Marco like T- shirts?   Yes, he _____ .

2. _____ Ping like red dresses?   Yes, she _____ .

3. _____ you like T-shirts?   Yes, I _____ .

4. _____ they want leather jackets?   Yes, they _____ .

5. _____ Jenny want new shoes?   Yes, she _____ .

6. _____ you and your classmates like new clothes?   Yes, we _____ .

7. _____ your teacher have a sweater?   Yes, ____ _____ .

8. What color shoes _____ your teacher like?

9. What color jeans _____ Tanya and Jenny like?

10. What color jeans _____ you have at home?

5 **Listen** Listen and complete the chart.

PING LIKES . . .	PING DOESN'T LIKE . . .

6 **Pair Practice** Work with a partner. Ask your partner questions about clothes Ping likes or doesn't like.

Example: Student 1: Does Ping like blue jeans?
Student 2: Yes, she does.

7 **Write** Read the receipt. Complete the conversation. Then practice the conversation with a partner.

THE downtown SHOPPER

1 pair blue jeans, size 8..........$59.00
1 pair ladies' shoes, brown....$89.00
1 silk blouse, black,
    size medium....................$75.00

subtotal............$223.00
tax....................$17.00
TOTAL.....$240.00

NO REFUNDS WITHOUT RECEIPT

A: What does Tanya have from the store?
B: She has a pair of ____ jeans, size ____ .
A: What else does she have?
B: She has a ____ of brown ____ .
A: What else?
B: She also has a ____ silk ____ , size ____ .
A: How much are the shoes?
B: _____ dollars.
A: How much is the total bill?
B: _____ dollars.
A: That's a lot of money!

8 **Write** Write a check for Tanya's new clothes.

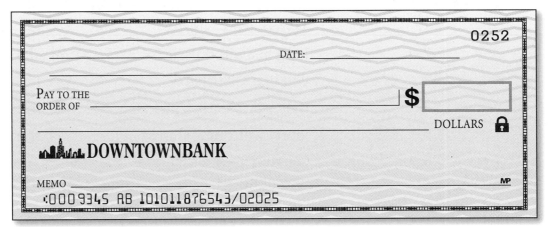

0252

DATE: _____

PAY TO THE
ORDER OF _____ $ [   ]

DOLLARS 🔒

DOWNTOWNBANK

MEMO _____ _____ MP
⑆0009345 AB 101011876543/02025

9 **Teamwork Task** Work in teams of three. Make a list of clothes you all like. Then make a list of clothes you don't like. (For example: "We like black shoes." "We don't like orange pants.") You must all agree on each item.

Game Time

Your teacher will write three clothing items on a receipt. Guess what they are. (Include the color and the kind of clothing.)

Review

1 Read and Listen Read the story. Listen to the story.

Winter Clothes

It is November. The weather is getting cold. Ping and Jenny are shopping together for winter clothes. Jenny wants a sweater. She wants a pink sweater. Ping doesn't like sweaters very much. But she needs something warm. She wants a jacket. She wants a warm jacket.

The sweaters are very nice. "What size do you need?" Ping asks. Jenny needs a small. "What color do you want?" Ping asks. Jenny wants pink. "This is a really nice one," Ping says. She picks up the sweater.

Jenny looks at it. "It looks great," she says. "But how much is it?"

"It's $89."

"That's too much," Jenny says. "I only have $50." Jenny wants to pay cash. She doesn't like credit cards. "There's a nice jacket," she says, pointing at a rack of jackets.

Ping picks up one jacket. It is warm and black, and it is beautiful. It is a size medium.

"How much is it?" Jenny asks.

"$149."

"That's a lot."

Ping tries on the jacket. It looks great. "It's not too much," she says. "I really like it!" Fortunately, Ping has a credit card.

2 Write Answer the questions.

1. What does Jenny want? _____

2. Does Jenny want a sweater? _____

3. Does Ping want a sweater? _____

4. What color sweater does Jenny want? _____

5. How much is the sweater? _____

6. How much money does Jenny have? _____

7. What size jacket does Ping need? _____

8. How much is the jacket? _____

9. Who has a credit card? _____

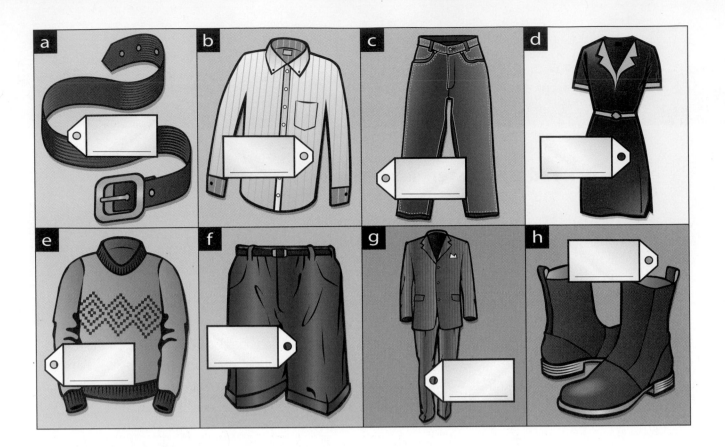

3 **Write** Write the name of each item.

a. _____

b. _____

c. _____

d. _____

e. _____

f. _____

g. _____

h. _____

4 **Listen** Listen and check your answers to Activity 3. Then write the prices in the picture.

5 Best Answer Bubble the correct answers.

	a	**b**	**c**

1. A five-cent coin is a _____.
   a) quarter   b) half dollar   c) nickel   ○ ○ ○

2. How much money does Marco have?
   He _____ twenty dollars.
   a) have   b) has   c) is   ○ ○ ○

3. How much _____ the dresses?
   a) are   b) is   c) has   ○ ○ ○

4. She wants a new _____ .
   a) blouse   b) shorts   c) pants   ○ ○ ○

5. I _____ like red shoes.
   a) no   b) don't   c) doesn't   ○ ○ ○

6. My teacher _____ sweaters.
   a) like   b) don't like   c) doesn't like   ○ ○ ○

6 Write Correct the mistakes. Write *correct* if the sentence is correct.

1. I like blues shoes. _____

2. He has a jacket black. _____

3. She want a yellow dress. _____

4. They need new socks. _____

5. He wants a brown shoes. _____

6. The pants are thirty dollars. _____

7. He have only twenty dollars. _____

8. I don't needs a suit. _____

9. They doesn't like red jackets. _____

10. What size do you need? I need a medium. _____

7 Pronunciation Plural nouns have three ending sounds: /s/, /z/, and /iz/. Listen and repeat.

/s/   pants, socks, boots
/z/   shoes, sweaters, jeans
/iz/ dresses, blouses, necklaces

Listen again and write the sound you hear (/s/, /z/, or /iz/).

shirts _____   shorts _____   credit cards _____   jackets _____   sizes _____

8 **Teamwork Task A.** Work in teams of four or five. Choose two volunteers. Ask the volunteers questions about what clothes they have at home. List all the clothes each volunteer has in the boxes below. Include colors. Don't ask the sizes!

Example: *Student 1:* Do you have any jackets?
Volunteer 1: Yes, I do.
Student 2: How many jackets do you have?
Volunteer 1: I have three jackets.
Student 3: What color jackets do you have?
Volunteer 1: I have a brown jacket, a blue jacket, and a black jacket.

VOLUNTEER 1	VOLUNTEER 2
three jackets—brown, blue, and black	

B. Work together to write sentences about your volunteers on a sheet of paper.

I can . . .			
• identify U.S. coins and bills.	1	2	3
• make purchases and count money.	1	2	3
• ask for and give prices.	1	2	3
• identify colors.	1	2	3
• identify types of clothing.	1	2	3
• describe clothing.	1	2	3
• express likes and dislikes.	1	2	3
• understand sizes.	1	2	3
• offer help.	1	2	3
• read a sales receipt.	1	2	3
• write a check.	1	2	3

1 = not well   2 = OK   3 = very well

Sales clerk: May I help you?
Tanya: Yes, please. Where (1) _____ the dresses?

Jenny: What (2) _____ do you (3) _____ ?
Tanya: Black. I (4) _____ black dresses.

Tanya: Look at this one. What do you think?
Ping: It's really nice. What (5) _____ is it?
Tanya: Size six.

Ping: That's too small. I (6) _____ a size eight, I think.
Tanya: Here's an eight.

Tanya: It looks great on you. How (7) _____ is it?
Ping: It's a lot. But I (8) _____ my credit card.

Ping: My husband (9) _____ black dresses. And he (10) _____ me to buy a nice dress.
Tanya: Lucky you!

10 **Group Practice** Work in groups of three. Practice the conversation. Student 1 is Tanya. Student 2 is Ping. Student 3 is the sales clerk.

Home and Family

GOALS

- ✓ Identify family members.
- ✓ Describe your family.
- ✓ Ask and answer questions about family.
- ✓ Write about your family.
- ✓ Complete a census form.
- ✓ Identify rooms in a house.
- ✓ Ask and answer questions about activities.
- ✓ Identify work activities.
- ✓ Use adjectives to describe people.

Jenny's Family

Ramon

Isabel

Andrea

Jenny

Francisco

Miguel · Luisa · Hector · Martha

1 **Listen** *Listen and repeat.*

1. father
2. mother
3. parents
4. grandfather
5. grandmother
6. uncle
7. aunt
8. brother
9. sister
10. husband
11. wife

2 **Pronunciation**

father	uncle
mother	brother
parents	sister
grandfather	husband
grandmother	

1 **Say It** Listen to the conversation. Say it with a partner.

Hi, Sis.

A: Who is that?
B: That's <u>Andrea</u>.
A: Who is <u>Andrea</u>?
B: <u>She</u> is Jenny's <u>sister</u>.

Andrea / sister

Practice more conversations. Use the pictures below.

Hi, Mom.

Hi, Dad.

Hi, Gram.

1. Isabel / mother   **2. Ramon / father**   **3. Martha / grandmother**

Ask more questions about Jenny's family. Use the picture on pages 82–83.

father   mother

daughter   son

2 **Write** Look at the picture on pages 82–83 and complete the sentences. Use these words: *daughter, son, brother, sister, mother, parents, father, children.*

1. Francisco is Jenny's brother. Jenny is Francisco's _____ .

2. Jenny is Isabel's daughter. Isabel is Jenny's _____ .

3. Jenny is Ramon's daughter. Ramon is Jenny's _____ .

4. Jenny, Francisco, and Andrea are Ramon's _____ .

5. Ramon and Isabel are Jenny's _____ .

6. Miguel is Ramon's _____ .

7. Francisco is Ramon and Isabel's _____ .

8. Jenny is Ramon and Isabel's _____ .

3 **Write** Answer the questions with names and relationships.

1. Who is he?

   He is Tanya's brother.

2. Who is she?

   _____

3. Who are they?

   _____

4. Who is he?

   _____

4 **Listen** Listen and write sentences about the family relationships.

1. She is Marco's mother. _____
2. _____
3. _____
4. _____
5. _____

5 Write Write the names of your family members in the circles. Add more circles for more family members.

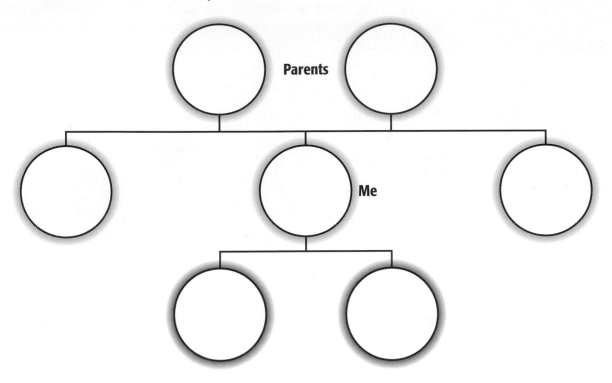

6 Pair Practice Work with a partner. Ask your partner questions about his or her family. Point to a circle.

Example: *Student 1:* Who is he?
Student 2: He is my father. His name is Oscar.

Culture Tip

Small families
The average home in the U.S. has 2.6 people living in it. How many people live in your home?

7 Write Write sentences about your family. Write as many as you can.

HE / SHE	I
Oscar is my father.	I am Oscar's son.

Now, write five sentences about your partner's family on a sheet of paper.

Pair Practice Work with a partner. Practice the conversation. Then complete the census form.

Census Form
Start Here

1. NAME	2. RELATIONSHIP TO HEAD	3. DATE OF BIRTH	4. AGE
Pedro Lopez	Head of Household	1/5/56	

A: Are you the head of household?

B: The head of household?

A: That's the person who pays the rent.

B: Yes, I am.

A: What's your name?

B: Pedro Lopez.

A: What is your date of birth?

B: January 5, 1956.

A: Who else lives in your home?

B: My wife. Her name is Olivia. O-L-I-V-I-A.

A: What is her date of birth?

B: Her date of birth is February 1, 1961.

A: Does anyone else live in your home?

B: Yes. My son, Marco, lives here. His name is Marco Lopez.

A: What is his date of birth?

B: He was born on March 2, 1985.

A: Anyone else?

B: No, that's all.

Game Time

Your teacher will write the name of a family member. Try to guess your teacher's relationship to the person.

Example: Is she your daughter? Is she your grandmother?

Home

Jenny's Home

 Kitchen

Living room

Dining room

Bathroom

Bedroom

Yard

1 Pronunciation Listen and repeat.

1. kitchen
2. living room
3. dining room
4. bathroom
5. bedroom
6. yard

2 **Pair Practice** Work with a partner. Ask and answer questions about Jenny's family on page 88.

Example: *Student 1:* Where is Jenny's mother?
Student 2: She is in the kitchen.

3 **Say It** Listen to the conversation. Say it with a partner.

taking a shower

A: What time is it?
B: It's <u>seven o'clock</u>.
A: Where is Ping?
B: She is in the <u>bathroom</u>.
A: What's she doing?
B: She is <u>taking a shower</u>.

Practice more conversations. Use the pictures below.

1. eating breakfast

2. washing the dishes

3. talking on the telephone

4. reading the newspaper

5. writing an e-mail

6. watching TV

Present continuous		
Subject	**be**	**Verb + -ing**
I	**am**	study**ing**
you	**are**	study**ing**
he/she/it	**is**	study**ing**
we	**are**	study**ing**
you	**are**	study**ing**
they	**are**	study**ing**

Check Points:

✓ Use the present continuous to talk about now.

  I am listening to my teacher now.

✓ Add -ing to most verbs to form the present continuous.

  study ⟶ **studying**

  For verbs that end in -e, drop the -e and add -ing.

  write ⟶ **writing**

4 **Write** Complete the sentences with present continuous verbs.

1. (watch) What's Ping doing?

   She _____ _____ television.

2. (listen) What is Carolina doing?

   She _____ _____ to music.

3. (take) What is Marco doing?

   He _____ _____ a shower.

4. (cook) What are Mr. and Mrs. Herrera doing?

   They _____ _____.

5. (buy) What is Tanya doing?

   _____ _____ _____ a dress.

6. (study) What are you doing?

   _____ _____ _____

7. (teach) What is your teacher doing?

   _____ _____ _____

8. (sleep) What are Grandma and Grandpa doing?

   _____ _____ _____

5 **Pair Practice** Work with a partner. Ask and answer the questions in Activity 4.

6 **Match** Complete the sentences. Write the letter.

1. __f__ She is watching ___ .   a. a shower.
2. ___ He is reading ___ .   b. the dishes.
3. ___ He is washing ___ .   c. on the telephone.
4. ___ They are talking ___ .   d. a letter.
5. ___ She is taking ___ .   e. a book.
6. ___ He is writing ___ .   f. TV.

7 **Listen** Listen and circle the word you hear.

1. bedroom   bathroom
2. reading   writing
3. talking   taking
4. washing   watching
5. talking   taking
6. bedroom   bathroom

8 **Write** Write sentences about you.

WHERE ARE YOU?	WHAT ARE YOU DOING?
1. I am in the bedroom.	I am sleeping.
2. I am in the kitchen.	
3. I am in the dining room.	
4. I am in the living room.	
5. _____	I am drinking coffee.
6. _____	I am brushing my teeth.
7. _____	I am doing my homework.
8. _____	I am reading the newspaper.
9. _____	I am cooking dinner.
10. _____	

⑨ Pair Practice Work with a partner. Ask and answer questions about Jenny's family members on page 88.

Example: *Student 1:* Where is Jenny's grandmother?
Student 2: She's in the living room.
Student 1: What is she doing?
Student 2: She's watching TV.

⑩ Group Practice Pretend you are at home right now. Answer these questions

1. Where are you? _____

2. What are you doing? _____

Now, walk around the room. Ask your classmates where they are and what they are doing. Write their names below.

_____ is in the kitchen.

_____ is in the living room.

_____ is in the bedroom.

_____ is in the dining room.

_____ is eating.

_____ is drinking.

_____ is watching TV.

_____ is cooking.

_____ is _____.

Game Time

Line up

Student 1: Stand up and tell where you are and what you are doing.

Example: I am in the kitchen. I am cooking.

Student 2: Stand behind Student 1. Tell where Student 1 is and what he or she is doing. Then tell where you are and what you are doing.

Example: He is in the kitchen. He is cooking. I am in the bedroom. I am sleeping.

Continue to add students until someone makes a mistake. The last student before the mistake wins!

What are they doing?

1 **Say It** Listen to the conversation. Say it with a partner.

Carlos / fix a car

A: Where is <u>Carlos</u>?
B: <u>He</u> is at work.
A: What is <u>he</u> doing?
B: <u>He is fixing a car</u>.

Practice more conversations. Use the pictures below.

1. **Alison / teach a class**

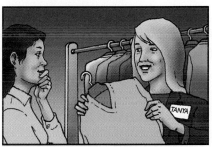

2. **Tanya / help a customer**

3. **Marco / cook chicken**

4. **Julia / cut hair**

5. **Ping / answer the phone**

6. **You / study English**

Present continuous questions and short answers

Question	Affirmative Answer	Negative Answer
Am I cook**ing?**	Yes, **you are.**	No, **you aren't.**
Are you cook**ing?**	Yes, **I am.**	No, **I'm not.**
Is he cook**ing?**	Yes, **he is.**	No, **he isn't.**
Is she cook**ing?**	Yes, **she is.**	No, **she isn't.**
Are we cook**ing?**	Yes, **we are.**	No, **we aren't.**
Are they cook**ing?**	Yes, **they are.**	No, **they aren't.**

Check Point:

✓ Contractions

No, he **isn't.** = No, **he's** not.
No, she **isn't.** = No, **she's** not.
No, you **aren't.** = No, **you're** not.
No, we **aren't.** = No, **we're** not.
No, they **aren't.** = No, **they're** not.

2 Say It Listen to the conversation. Say it with a partner.

A: Is <u>Ping</u> in the kitchen?
B: Yes, <u>she</u> is.
A: Is <u>she</u> <u>cooking</u>?
B: No, <u>she</u> isn't. <u>She</u> is <u>drinking tea</u>.

cooking? / drinking tea

Practice more conversations. Use the pictures below.

1. sleeping? / studying English

2. taking a shower? /
brushing his teeth

3. watching TV? /
using her computer

3 Say It Listen to the conversation. Say it with a partner.

A: Where are <u>my parents</u>?
B: <u>They're</u> in the <u>living room</u>.
A: Are <u>they</u> <u>watching a movie</u>?
B: No, <u>they aren't</u>. <u>They're</u> <u>watching the news</u>.

my parents / watching a movie? /
watching the news

Practice more conversations. Use the pictures below.

1. my aunt and uncle / cooking? /
drinking tea and talking

2. my children / sleeping? /
listening to music and dancing

3. my grandparents / watering
flowers? / resting

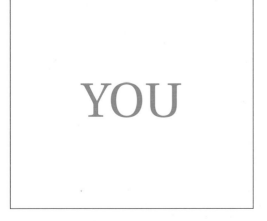

YOU

4. studying mathematics? / ?

4 Say It Listen to the conversation. Say it with a partner.

A: Tell me about <u>Ping's husband</u>. Is <u>he</u> <u>tall or short</u>?

B: <u>He's</u> <u>tall</u>.

A: How <u>tall</u> is <u>he</u>?

B: <u>He's</u> very <u>tall</u>.

Ping's husband / tall or short?

Practice more conversations. Use the pictures below.

1. Han's wife / thin or heavy?

2. Monica's grandfather / old or young?

3. Tanya's boyfriend / handsome or ugly?

5 Teamwork Task Work in teams of three or four. Complete the sentences. Use names of people in your family or famous people.

1. _____ is very tall.

2. _____ is short.

3. _____ is thin.

4. _____ is very old.

5. _____ is very handsome. (a man)

6. _____ is very beautiful. (a woman)

 Read and Listen Read the story. Listen to the story.

Happy Anniversary

Today is Jenny's mother and father's 25th wedding anniversary and they are having a party. All of the people in Jenny's family are attending the party except Jenny. Jenny isn't in Colombia. She is living in California. She is going to school and studying English in Los Angeles.

In Colombia, Jenny's father is in the yard. He is cooking chicken for everyone on the barbecue grill. Jenny's Aunt Luisa is talking to everyone and putting dishes on the table. Jenny's sister, Andrea, is making a chocolate cake for the party. Her daughter, Karla, is helping her. Jenny's grandparents are in the living room. They are sitting on the couch and watching TV.

Right now, Jenny's mom is talking on the telephone. She is talking to her daughter in California. She is talking to Jenny.

"I'm sorry I'm not there with you," Jenny says, "but I'm calling to wish you a happy anniversary."

Jenny's mom is smiling. She is smiling because she is looking at her family around her and she is talking to her other daughter on the telephone. "Thank you for calling," Jenny's mom says. "We all miss you."

"I miss you, too, " Jenny says.

✏ **Write** Read the sentences. Circle *true* or *false*. Correct the false sentences to make them true.

1.	Today is Jenny's parents' 25th birthday.	True	False
2.	Jenny is in Colombia studying English.	True	False
3.	Jenny's father is cooking.	True	False
4.	Jenny's aunt is talking a lot.	True	False
5.	Jenny's daughter is making a chocolate cake.	True	False
6.	Jenny's parents are watching TV.	True	False
7.	Jenny is talking to her mother on the phone.	True	False
8.	Jenny's mother is angry because she is talking to her daughter in California.	True	False

3 Write Write sentences about the people in the picture. Tell what they are doing.

a. _____

b. _____

c. _____

d. _____

e. _____

f. _____

g. _____

h. _____

4 Listen Listen and write the sentences.

1. _____

2. _____

3. _____

4. _____

5. _____

6. _____

⑤ Best Answer Bubble the correct answers.

	a	b	c	d

1. Alicia is my sister. I am her _____ .
   a) daughter   b) brother
   c) nephew   d) husband
   ○ ○ ○ ○

2. Is she old? No, she isn't. She's _____ .
   a) short   b) young
   c) rich   d) heavy
   ○ ○ ○ ○

3. What's she doing? She's _____ lunch.
   a) cook   b) eating
   c) washing   d) doing
   ○ ○ ○ ○

4. What's he doing? He's _____ the dishes.
   a) watching   b) washing
   c) playing   d) cooking
   ○ ○ ○ ○

5. What are they doing? They _____ .
   a) are cook   b) sleeping
   c) watching TV   d) are working
   ○ ○ ○ ○

⑥ Write Correct the mistakes in the sentences. If there are no mistakes, write *correct*.

1. He's take a shower. _____

2. She is sleeping. _____

3. Is she listen to music? _____

4. They cooking dinner. _____

5. They're studying English. _____

6. Are they eat dinner right now? _____

7. No, they are. _____

8. Do you listening to the teacher now? _____

⑦ Pronunciation Listen and repeat the sentences. Stress the correct syllables.

1. He's cooking dinner.
2. She's taking a shower.
3. They're watching television.
4. He's washing the dishes.
5. She's listening to music.

8 **Teamwork Task** Work in teams of five.

A. Pretend you are in a big house right now. Tell your teammates where you are and what you are doing. Everyone chooses a different room and activity.

Example: I am in the kitchen. I am cooking.

B. Write two sentences about each of your teammates.

Example: Marco is in the bathroom. He is taking a shower.

_____

_____

_____

_____

_____

C. Close your books. Choose a team leader. The team leader will tell your teacher where your teammates are and what they are doing.

I can . . .			
• identify family members.	1	2	3
• describe my family.	1	2	3
• ask and answer questions about family.	1	2	3
• write about my family.	1	2	3
• complete a census form.	1	2	3
• identify rooms in a house.	1	2	3
• ask and answer questions about activities.	1	2	3
• identify work activities.	1	2	3
• use adjectives to describe people.	1	2	3

1 = not well   2 = OK   3 = very well

DOWNTOWN

9 **Write** Write the missing words in the story. Use these words: *brother, family's, is, are, living, working, having, sleeping, teaching, doing.*

Jenny: Where is your family now, Tanya?
Tanya: Well, my (1) _____ is here in L.A. He's (2) _____ at a movie studio.

Jenny: That's interesting. How about you, Ping? Where is your family?
Ping: My brother (3) _____ (4) _____ in New York. He's working at a bank.

Ping: The rest of my family is in China. I'm sure they (5) _____ (6) _____ right now. It's very late in China right now.

Ping: But my husband is here. That's the most important thing. He's (7) _____ at the university.
Jenny: That's great. Teaching college is a very good job.

Tanya: How about you, Jenny? What's your family (8) _____ right now?
Jenny: Right now, they are all at my (9) _____ home in Colombia.

Jenny: They are (10) _____ a party for my parents' wedding anniversary. Right now, I miss them a lot.
Tanya: Sometimes I miss my family, too.
Ping: Me, too.

10 **Group Practice** Work in groups of three. Practice the conversation. Student 1 is Jenny. Student 2 is Tanya. Student 3 is Ping.

Housing

GOALS

- ✓ Identify furniture and appliances.
- ✓ Ask and answer questions about furniture and appliances.
- ✓ Use *there is* and *there are* to describe locations in a house.
- ✓ Write about a living room.
- ✓ Describe items at a garage sale.
- ✓ Complain about housing problems.
- ✓ Read housing ads.
- ✓ Understand abbreviations in housing ads.
- ✓ Ask about an apartment for rent.
- ✓ Compare types of housing.
- ✓ Request service from utility companies.

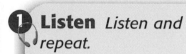

1 Listen *Listen and repeat.*

1. a sofa / a couch
2. a coffee table
3. an armchair
4. a rug
5. a TV
6. a stove
7. a refrigerator
8. a dishwasher
9. cabinets
10. a bed
11. a night table
12. a lamp
13. a dresser
14. a mirror
15. curtains
16. a sink
17. a shower
18. a toilet

2 Pronunciation

• sofa	• dresser
• armchair	• mirror
• carpet	• curtains
• refrigerator	• shower
• dishwasher	• toilet
• cabinets	

At Home

 Say It Listen to the conversation. Say it with a partner.

A: What's that?

B: It's <u>a lamp</u>.

A: Where is it?

B: It's in the <u>bedroom</u>.

A: There's <u>a lamp</u> in my <u>bedroom</u>, too.

a lamp

Practice more conversations. Use the pictures below.

1. a stove

2. a coffee table

3. a dresser

4. an armchair

GRAMMAR CHECK

There is / There are

Use *There is . . .* or *There are . . .* to describe the location of something.

We say: **There is** *a stove in my kitchen.* OR **There are** *chairs in my kitchen.*
We don't say: *A stove is in my kitchen.* OR *Chairs are in my kitchen.*

Check Point:
 ✓ You can use a contraction for *there is.* **There is = There's**

Is there / Are there

Question	Affirmative	Negative
Is there a bookcase in your living room?	Yes, *there is.*	No, *there isn't.*
Are there any books in the bookcase?	Yes, *there are.*	No, *there aren't.*

Check Point:
✓ Use *any* in questions and negative statements.

2 Say It Listen to the conversation. Say it with a partner.

A: Is there a <u>sofa</u> in your <u>living room</u>?

B: Yes, there is. There's a very nice <u>sofa</u> in my <u>living room</u>. Is there a <u>sofa</u> in your <u>living room</u>?

A: Yes, there is. *OR* No, there isn't.

sofa / living room

Practice more conversations. Use the pictures below.

1. **coffee table / living room**

2. **mirror / bathroom**

3. **dresser / bedroom**

4. **dishwasher / kitchen**

5. **microwave oven / kitchen**

6. **bathtub / bathroom**

3 Say It Listen to the conversation. Say it with a partner.

A: Are there any <u>cabinets</u> in your <u>kitchen</u>?

B: Yes, there are. Are there any <u>cabinets</u> in your <u>kitchen</u>?

A: Yes, there are. *OR* No, there aren't.

cabinets / kitchen

Practice more conversations. Use the pictures below.

1. **curtains / living room**

2. **lamps / bedroom**

3. **windows / kitchen**

4 Write Complete the sentences with *There is, There are, Is there,* or *Are there.*

1. _____ a swimming pool in the yard?

2. _____ any windows in the bathroom?

3. _____ a large kitchen in the apartment?

4. _____ several cabinets in the kitchen.

5. _____ a very nice shower in the bathroom.

6. _____ three bedrooms in the apartment.

5 Listen Listen and write the furniture and appliances in the correct rooms below.

KITCHEN	BEDROOM	BATHROOM	LIVING ROOM

6 **Pair Practice** Work with a partner. Ask and answer questions about Ping's living room.

Example: *Student 1:* Is there a coffee table in Ping's living room?
Student 2: Yes, there is.
Student 1: Where is it?
Student 2: It's in front of the sofa.

7 **Teamwork Task** Work in teams of three or four. Close your books. Write about Ping's living room. Write what is in the living room and where it is. Write as many sentences as you can on a sheet of paper.

Example: There is a coffee table in front of the sofa.

GRAMMAR CHECK

Articles: *a/an*

Use *a* or *an* with most singular nouns the first time you talk about them.
I have **a** sofa in my living room. There is **a** bed in my bedroom.
Use *an* when the next word starts with a vowel. (*A, E, I, O, U*)
an apartment, **an** old stove

Check Point:
✓ Don't use *a* or *an* with plural nouns.
~~a books~~

1 Say It Listen to the conversation. Say it with a partner.

A: Is there a <u>stove</u> in Tanya's apartment?
B: Yes, there is.
A: Is it <u>new</u> or <u>old</u>?
B: It's <u>old</u>. It's very <u>old</u>.
A: What does Tanya want?
B: She wants a <u>new</u> <u>stove</u>.

new or old?

Practice more conversations. Use the pictures below.

1. large or small?

2. beautiful or ugly?

3. expensive or cheap?

2 Write Write the correct article: *a* or *an*.

1. _____ kitchen
2. _____ old stove
3. _____ house
4. _____ apartment
5. _____ new apartment
6. _____ beautiful sofa
7. _____ expensive sofa
8. _____ ugly rug

3 Pronunciation
When we use the article *an*, we usually link, or connect, the *-n* to the beginning of the next word. Listen and repeat the linked pronunciation.

an apartment = a napartment

an old stove = a nold stove

an expensive rug = a nexpensive rug

4 Listen
Listen and write the articles and adjectives.

1. _____ living room
2. _____ kitchen
3. _____ bathroom
4. _____ cabinets
5. _____ yard
6. _____ rug

5 Write
Answer the questions with complete sentences.

1. Do you live in a house or an apartment?

   I live in . . .

2. Docs your home have a new stove or an old stove?

   _____

3. Do you have a cheap TV or an expensive TV?

   _____

4. Does your home have a beautiful bathroom or an ugly bathroom?

   _____

5. Do you have quiet neighbors or noisy neighbors?

   _____

6 Say It Listen to the conversation. Say it with a partner.

A: What's the matter?

B: I want to move. I want a new apartment.

A: Why? What's wrong with your apartment?

B: It's too <u>dark</u>. I want an apartment with <u>more light</u>.

dark / more light

Practice more conversations. Use the pictures below.

1. **small / large rooms**

2. **hot / air-conditioning**

3. **noisy / quiet neighbors**

7 Write Match the adjectives with their opposites.

_____ 1. dark   **a.** large

_____ 2. expensive   **b.** quiet

_____ 3. small   **c.** cheap

_____ 4. ugly   **d.** modern

_____ 5. dangerous   **e.** beautiful

_____ 6. noisy   **f.** clean

_____ 7. old-fashioned   **g.** light

_____ 8. dirty   **h.** safe

Listen Listen and write the prices.

9 **Pair Practice** Work with a partner. Pretend your partner is at the garage sale. Ask questions about the things at the garage sale.

Example: *Student 1:* Is there a dresser at the garage sale?
Student 2: Yes, there is.
Student 1: What does it look like?
Student 2: It's large and white. It looks old and ugly.
Student 1: How much is it?
Student 2: It's twenty dollars. Do you want it?
Student 1: Yes, I think so. *OR* No, I don't think so.

Say It Listen to the conversation. Say it with a partner.

A: Hello. This is Tanya in Apartment 301.

B: Hello, Tanya. What can I do for you?

A: <u>There isn't any heat</u> in my apartment.

B: <u>Heat</u>?

A: Yes. <u>There isn't any heat</u>.

B: OK. I'll come right over.

A: Thank you.

heat

Practice more conversations. Use the pictures below.

1. gas

2. clogged

3. leaking

11 **Teamwork Task** Work in teams of three or four. Choose a volunteer. Ask questions about the volunteer's living room.

Example: *Student 1:* What is in your living room?
Volunteer: There's a sofa in my living room.
Student 2: What does it look like?
Volunteer: It's large and brown.
Student 3: Where is it?
Volunteer: It's next to the door.

Write sentences about the volunteer's living room on a sheet of paper.

Example: There is a large brown sofa in José's living room.

Game Time

Your teacher will write the name of something in his or her home. Try to guess what it is. Ask *yes/no* questions. If the answer is "Yes," ask another question. If the answer is "No," another student asks.

Example: *Student 1:* Is it in the living room?   *Teacher:* Yes, it is.
            Student 1: Is it large?   *Teacher:* No, it isn't.

A New Apartment

> **Note:** **Definite article (*the*)**
>
> Use *the*, not *a/an*, when you are talking about one specific thing.
>
> I'm interested in **an** apartment for rent. = There are many apartments available for rent.
>
> I'm interested in **the** apartment for rent. = There is only one apartment for rent.

1 **Say It** Listen to the conversation. Say it with a partner.

A: I'm interested in the apartment for rent. Can I ask a question about it?

B: Sure.

A: Is there <u>a swimming pool</u>?

B: No, I'm afraid there isn't. Sorry.

a swimming pool

Practice more conversations. Use the pictures below.

1. a laundry room

2. a security gate

3. a garage or parking space

4. an exercise room

2 Read Read the ad.

Apt. For Rent
★ ★
unfurn.
2 BD, 2 BA, DR,
large kit. and 2 car gar.
$950 / mo. + $500 sec. dep.
Call (818) 555-8330.

3 Write Match the abbreviations in the ad to the words below.
Find abbreviations in the ad that match the words below.

1. bedroom _____
2. kitchen _____
3. garage _____
4. bathroom _____
5. dining room _____
6. apartment _____
7. month _____
8. security _____
9. unfurnished _____
10. deposit _____

Culture Tip

Furnished or unfurnished?

Unfurnished means that the house or apartment has no furniture. You have to buy or bring furniture. *Furnished* means that a place for rent already has some furniture. Most houses and apartments for rent are unfurnished.

4 **Say It** Listen to the conversation. Say it with a partner.

pool?

A: Hello. I'm calling about the apartment for rent. Is it still available?

B: Yes, it is.

A: How many bedrooms does it have?

B: It has <u>two bedrooms and one bathroom</u>.

A: Is there a <u>pool</u>?

B: Yes, there is.

A: How much is the rent?

B: It's <u>$1,200</u> a month. Do you want to see it?

A: Yes, please.

Practice more conversations. Use the ads below.

1. **a laundry room?**

2. **a big yard?**

3. **a parking space?**

5 **Listen** Listen and write the missing information in the ads.

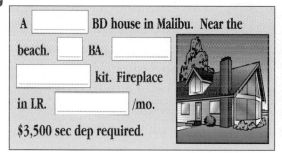

1.

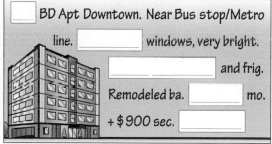

2.

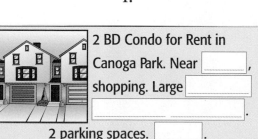

3.

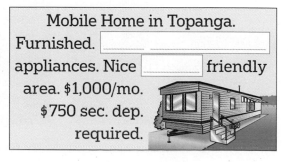

4.

6 Group Practice Work in groups of four. Each student picks one of the homes in Activity 4. Pretend you want to live there. Student 1: Tell your classmates about the home you like. Tell as much information as you can. Student 2: Pick a different home. Tell your classmates about it. Student 3 and 4 must pick a different home.

7 Teamwork Task Work in teams of four. Decide which home in Activity 4 is the best home for Tanya. Write why you like this home.

_____

_____

_____

_____

8 Say It Listen to the conversation. Say it with a partner.

Water Department / **water**

A: Good morning. <u>Water Department</u>.

B: Hello. I'm calling because I need to turn on my <u>water</u> service.

A: Is this a new account?

B: Yes, it is.

A: How about tomorrow afternoon? Will you be home tomorrow afternoon?

B: Yes, tomorrow afternoon is fine.

A: OK. What's your address?

Practice more conversations. Use the pictures below.

1. **Gas Company / gas**

2. **Electric Company / electric**

3. **Telephone Company / telephone**

1 🎧 **Read and Listen** Read the story. Listen to the story.

Home

Ping is happy with her home. She lives in a two-bedroom house in a safe, quiet neighborhood. Her house has a large kitchen and a modern bathroom. There are four large windows in her living room and there is a swimming pool in her yard.

Tanya isn't happy with her apartment. There is only one bedroom. The bathroom is small and the kitchen is old. There isn't a swimming pool. And there aren't many windows. In fact, there is only one small window in her bedroom so her bedroom isn't very bright. And her neighbors are noisy.

Ping likes her home so she doesn't want to move. But Tanya isn't happy with her apartment. She wants a new place to live. She wants to be happy.

2 **Write** Circle *true* or *false*.

1.	Ping likes her house.	True	False
2.	There are three bedrooms in Ping's house.	True	False
3.	There is a large kitchen in Ping's house.	True	False
4.	Ping's bathroom is old.	True	False
5.	Ping's living room is dark.	True	False
6.	Tanya likes her home.	True	False
7.	Tanya lives in a large apartment.	True	False
8.	Tanya's kitchen is modern.	True	False
9.	Tanya's bedroom is dark.	True	False
10.	Tanya wants to move.	True	False

3 Write Write sentences about the things in this living room. Use prepositions. Write as many sentences as you can on a sheet of paper.

Example: There is a TV in the entertainment center.

4 Listen and Write Write the sentences you hear. Don't forget periods (.) and question marks (?).

1. _____

2. _____

3. _____

4. _____

5. _____

5 Best Answer Bubble the correct answers.

	a	b	c	d
	○	○	○	○

1. There _____ some cabinets in my kitchen.
   a) are   **b)** aren't
   c) is   **d)** isn't

2. The couch is _____ the coffee table.
   a) in   **b)** on
   c) in front of **d)** under

3. The bedroom isn't very bright. It's really _____ .
   a) dark   **b)** beautiful
   c) large   **d)** expensive

4. Is it still available? Yes, _____ .
   a) they are   **b)** there is
   c) it is   **d)** it does

5. Is the kitchen large or _____?
   a) ugly   **b)** big
   c) expensive   **d)** small

6. The bathroom isn't beautiful. In fact, it's _____ .
   a) ugly   **b)** big
   c) new   **d)** expensive

6 Write Correct the mistakes in the sentences. Write *correct* if there are no mistakes.

1. Are there a lamp in your bedroom? _____

2. It is new or old? _____

3. There is a beautiful carpet in their living room. _____

4. There is some stove in the kitchen. _____

5. There are any curtains in your living room? _____

6. How many parking spaces is there? _____

7 Pronunciation With *or* questions, the voice should go up with the first choice and down with the second choice. Listen and practice the questions.

Is it new or old?   Are they cheap or expensive?

Is it small or large?   Is the bedroom dark or bright?

8 **Write** Read the ad. Write sentences about the apartment on a sheet of paper.

Apartment for Rent

2 BD, 1 BA, pool,
lg yard with fruit trees,
new carpets, modern kit,
Venice,
$1,050/mo.

9 **Teamwork Task** Work in teams of three or four. Create an ad for your dream home. How many bedrooms and bathrooms does it have? What is the location? What else does it have? How much is the rent?

I can . . .			
• identify furniture and appliances.	1	2	3
• ask and answer questions about furniture and appliances.	1	2	3
• use *there is* and *there are* to describe locations in a house.	1	2	3
• write about a living room.	1	2	3
• describe items at a garage sale.	1	2	3
• complain about housing problems.	1	2	3
• read housing ads.	1	2	3
• understand abbreviations in housing ads.	1	2	3
• ask about an apartment for rent.	1	2	3
• compare types of housing.	1	2	3
• request service from utility companies.	1	2	3

1 = not well   2 = OK   3 = very well

10 **Write** Write the missing words in the story. Use these words: *Is, are, available, many, bright, modern, expensive, there, living room, small.*

Tanya: Is the two-bedroom apartment still (1) _____ ?
Manager: Yes, it is.

Tanya: How (2) _____ bathrooms does it have?
Manager: There (3) _____ two bathrooms. And there is a very nice (4) _____ .

Ping: (5) _____ there a swimming pool?
Manager: No, I'm afraid (6) _____ isn't.

Tanya: Are the bedroom windows large or (7) _____ ?
Manager: There are two large windows in each bedroom. The bedrooms are very (8) _____ .

Ping: How about the kitchen? Is it (9) _____ or old-fashioned?
Manager: It's new. It's a new kitchen with all new appliances.

Tanya: I like it, but it's (10) _____ .
Ping: You need a nice place to live, Tanya. That's really important.
Tanya: You're right. I'll take it!

11 **Group Practice** Work in groups of three. Practice the conversation. Student 1 is Tanya. Student 2 is Ping. Student 3 is the apartment manager.

The Community

GOALS

✓ Identify places in the community.

✓ Describe locations.

✓ Ask for and give directions.

✓ Identify service agencies in the community.

✓ Identify postal services.

✓ Identify banking services.

✓ Fill out a bank deposit slip.

✓ Read destination signs on buses.

✓ Write about your neighborhood.

✓ Compare two neighborhoods.

✓ Identify jobs and workplaces in the community.

✓ Describe job duties.

✓ Talk about habitual activities.

① Listen *Listen and repeat.*

1. a post office
2. a library
3. a bank
4. a police station
5. a movie theater
6. a supermarket
7. a drugstore
8. a gas station
9. a hospital
10. a café
11. an apartment building
12. a school
13. a fire station
14. a park

② Pronunciation

- library
- supermarket
- hospital
- café
- apartment

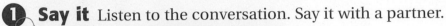

1 Say it Listen to the conversation. Say it with a partner.

post office

A: Is there a <u>post office</u> in Tanya's new neighborhood?

B: Yes, there is.

A: Where is it?

B: It's on <u>Third Avenue</u> next to the <u>library</u>.

Practice more conversations. Use the pictures below.

1. bank

2. supermarket

2 Pair Practice Work with a partner. Ask and answer questions about Tanya's neighborhood on pages 122–123.

Example: *Student 1:* Is there a gas station in Tanya's neighborhood?"
Student 2: Yes, there is.
Student 1: Where is it?
Student 2: It's on Main Street next to the hospital.

3 Pair Practice Work with a different partner. Ask and answer questions about your partner's neighborhood.

Example: *Student 1:* Is there a gas station in your neighborhood?"
Student 2: Yes, there is.
Student 1: Where is it?
Student 2: It's on _____ next to _____ .

Word Help: Directions

Turn left.   Turn right.   Go straight.

4 **Say it** Listen to the conversation. Say it with a partner.

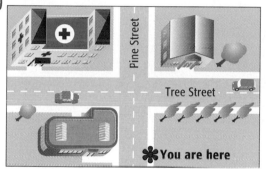

hospital

A: Is there a <u>hospital</u> in this neighborhood?

B: Yes, there is.

A: Where is it?

B: <u>It's on Tree Street. Go up Pine Street to Tree Street. Turn left on Tree Street</u>. You can't miss it.

A: Thank you.

Practice more conversations. Use the pictures below.

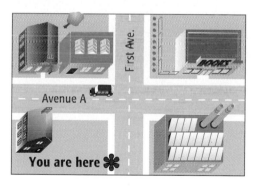

1. bookstore

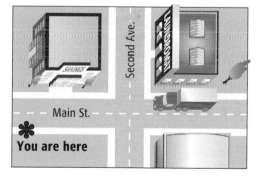

2. laundromat

GRAMMAR CHECK

Imperative

The imperative is the base form of a verb. Use the imperative to give directions or commands.

    Go up Third Street. **Turn** right on First Avenue.

5 Listen Listen and write the places on the map: *drugstore, supermarket, adult school, library.*

JENNY'S NEIGHBORHOOD

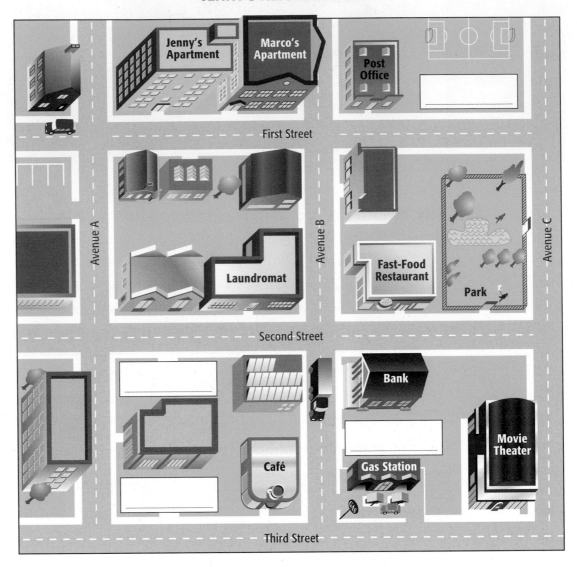

6 Pair Practice Work with a partner. Ask and answer questions about Jenny's neighborhood.

Example: *Student 1:* Is there a movie theater in Jenny's neighborhood?
Student 2: Yes, there is. It's on Third Street.
Student 1: How can I get there from the supermarket?
Student 2: Go straight on Third Street. You can't miss it.

7 Write Complete the sentences with a place in Jenny's neighborhood.

1. _The supermarket_ is on Third Street next to the café.
2. _____ is on the corner of Second Street and Avenue A.
3. _____ is across the street from the fast-food restaurant.
4. _____ is on First Street next to the post office.
5. _____ is between the gas station and the bank.
6. _____ is on First Street near Avenue A.
7. _____ is on the corner of Second Street and Avenue C.

8 Teamwork Task Work in teams of three or four. List places in your community. Write what street they are on. What are they next to or near?

Include a post office, a hospital or clinic, a bank, a supermarket, a drugstore, a school, and four more places.

PLACE	STREET	NEXT TO _or_ NEAR

Game Time

Your teacher is thinking about a place in the neighborhood. Guess what it is.

Example: *Student 1:* Is it a movie theater?
Teacher: No, it isn't.
Student 2: Is it a . . . ?

The Neighborhood

① Say it Listen to the conversation. Say it with a partner.

an English book

A: Where are you?
B: I'm at the <u>library</u>.
A: What are you doing there?
B: I'm getting <u>an English book</u>.
A: Oh. That's a good idea.

Practice more conversations. Use the pictures below.

1. **a birthday cake**

2. **some stamps**

3. **a flu shot**

GRAMMAR CHECK

a, an, some

Use *a* or *an* for singular count nouns—things you can easily count.
a book, **a** dog, **an** apple
Use *some* for plural nouns or noncount nouns—things you can't easily count.
some cookies, **some** books, **some** water, **some** rice

② Write Complete the sentences with *a*, *an*, or *some*.

1. I need _____ car.
2. I need _____ apartment.
3. I need _____ groceries.
4. I need _____ haircut.
5. There is _____ hospital in my neighborhood.
6. There are _____ trees on my street.
7. There is _____ gas station on the corner.
8. There is _____ gas in my gas tank.

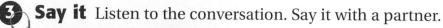

3 **Say it** Listen to the conversation. Say it with a partner.

get a haircut

A: Where are you going?
B: I'm going to the <u>beauty salon</u>.
A: Why are you going there?
B: I need to <u>get a haircut</u>.
A: That's a good reason.

Practice more conversations. Use the pictures below.

1. cash a check

2. get some groceries

3. wash my clothes

4. get some gas

5. fill a prescription

6. get some flowers

4 Write Read the list of things to do. Where can you do these things? Write them under the correct place.

Cash a check	Make a deposit	Get a money order
Pick up a package	Get a loan	Get a credit card
Get a change of address form	Make a withdrawal	Get a passport
Buy stamps		

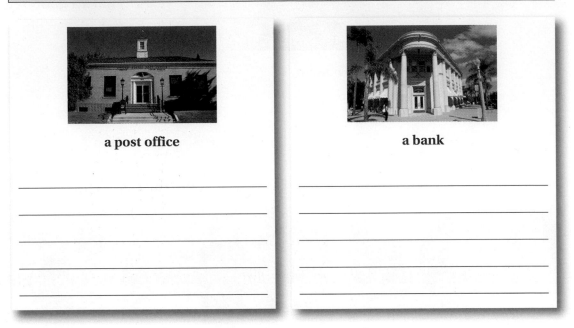

a post office

_____

_____

_____

_____

a bank

_____

_____

_____

_____

5 Pair Practice Work with a partner. Tell your partner what you need to do. Use the ideas in Activity 4. Your partner will tell you where to go.

Example: *Student 1:* I need to cash a check.
Student 2: Go to the bank. You can cash a check at the bank.

6 Write Fill out the bank deposit slip.

You have a check for one hundred and fourteen dollars and forty-two cents.
You have eighty-one dollars in cash.
Your checking account number is 12745-3386.

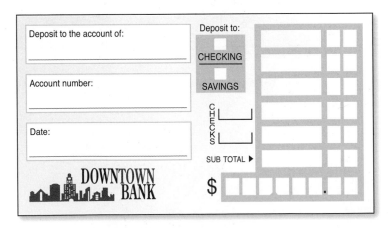

Deposit to the account of:

_____

Account number:

_____

Date:

Deposit to:

CHECKING

SAVINGS

C H E C K S

SUB TOTAL ▶

DOWNTOWN BANK

$

7 **Say It** Listen to the conversation. Say it with a partner.

Pacific Avenue

A: Excuse me. I want to go to <u>Venice Beach</u>. Which bus goes there?

B: Take Bus <u>28</u>. The number <u>28</u> bus goes to Venice Beach.

A: Where do I get off?

B: Get off at <u>Pacific Avenue</u>.

A: Thanks a lot.

Practice more conversations. Use the pictures below.

1. **Main Street**

2. **Ocean Avenue**

3. **Melrose Place**

8 **Write** Write directions from your school to your home. Write directions by bus. Write where you get on and get off. Then write directions by car or on foot.

1. By bus: _____

_____

_____

_____

_____

2. By car or on foot: _____

_____

_____

_____

_____

9 **Write** Write about places in your neighborhood. Use *there is, there are,* or *there isn't.*

Example: post office? There is a post office in my neighborhood. OR There are two post offices in my neighborhood. OR There isn't a post office in my neighborhood.

1. post office? _____

2. supermarket? _____

3. bank? _____

4. laundromat? _____

5. hospital? _____

6. park? _____

7. bookstore? _____

8. school? _____

9. drugstore? _____

10. restaurant? _____

10 **Pair Practice** Work with a partner. Ask questions about your partner's neighborhood.

Example: *Student 1:* Is there a supermarket in your neighborhood?
Student 2: Yes, there are two supermarkets in my neighborhood.
Student 1: Where are they?
Student 2: There is a supermarket on Venice Avenue and there is a supermarket on Main Street.

11 **Group Practice** Work with a large group or the whole class. Look at the picture on pages 122–123. Pretend you are somewhere in Tanya's neighborhood. Write the place.

Place: _____

Now, ask your classmates where they are in Tanya's neighborhood. Complete the chart.

NAME	PLACE		NAME	PLACE

Neighborhood Jobs

1 **Say It** Listen to the conversation. Say it with a partner.

clothing store / salesperson

A: Where is <u>Tanya</u>?

B: <u>She's</u> at work.

A: Where does <u>she</u> work?

B: <u>She</u> works in a <u>clothing store</u>. <u>She's</u> a <u>salesperson</u>.

Practice more conversations. Use the pictures below.

1. school / teacher

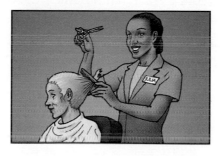

2. beauty salon / hair stylist

3. café / cashier

4. restaurant / cook

5. clinic / receptionist

6. gas station / mechanic

GRAMMAR CHECK

Simple present for jobs

Use the verb *be* to tell job titles.

I **am** a teacher. She **is** a doctor. They **are** lawyers.

Use the simple present to tell places of work.

He **works** in a school. She **works** in a bank. They **work** in a hospital.

2 **Listen and Write** Listen to the sentences. Do you hear a place or a job or both? Write the places and jobs you hear.

1. Place _____bank_____   Job _____
2. Place _____   Job _____
3. Place _____   Job _____
4. Place _____   Job _____
5. Place _____   Job _____
6. Place _____   Job _____

GRAMMAR CHECK

Simple present for habitual activities

Use the simple present for habitual activities. These are things you do every day, every week, every weekend, every summer, etc.

Subject	Verb	
I	work	in a bank.
You	cut	hair.
He	cooks	every day.
She	teaches	English.
We	fix	cars.
They	work	at a hospital.

doctor

3 **Write** Circle the correct verbs.

1. A doctor (work / works) in a hospital.
2. Several cashiers (work / works) in the supermarket.
3. An English teacher (teach / teaches) English.
4. Teachers usually (work / works) in schools.
5. A salesperson (sell / sells) things.
6. He (is / works) a salesperson.
7. Bus drivers (drive / drives) buses.
8. An auto mechanic (fix / fixes) cars.
9. They (work / works) in a restaurant.
10. My two brothers (work / are) servers in a restaurant.

bus driver

4 Say It Listen to the conversation. Say it with a partner.

A: What does <u>she</u> do?
B: <u>She's</u> a <u>hair stylist</u>.
A: What do <u>hair stylists</u> do?
B: They <u>cut hair</u>.

hair stylist / cut hair

Practice more conversations. Use the pictures below.

1. **doctor / help sick people**   2. **receptionist / answer phones and greet people**   3. **bus driver / drive buses**

Note: Spelling rules

Simple present verbs end in *-s* when the subject is *he, she,* or *it.*
For most verbs, add *-s* to the verb.
  I **cook** dinner. He **cooks** dinner.
For verbs that end in *ch, sh, s, x,* or *z,* add *-es.*
  I **wash** dishes. She **washes** dishes.
For verbs that end in a consonant + *y,* change *y* to *i* and add *-es.*
  I **study** English. He **studies** English.

---

5 Write Change the plural sentences to singular. Use the spelling rules.

1. English teachers teach English.   An English teacher <u>teaches</u> English.
2. Good students study every day.   A good student _____ every day.
3. Auto mechanics fix cars.   An auto mechanic _____ cars.
4. Cashiers count money.   A cashier _____ money.
5. Mail carriers carry the mail.   A mail carrier _____ mail.
6. Bank tellers cash checks.   A bank teller _____ checks.
7. Parking attendants park cars.   A parking attendant _____ cars.
8. Taxi drivers drive taxis.   A taxi driver _____ a taxi.

6 Pronunciation Verbs that end in -s are pronounced three different ways: /s/, /z/, or /iz/

Listen and repeat the verbs. Listen to the ending sound.

/s/:	works	cooks	cuts
/z/:	serves	gives	drives
/iz/:	fixes	teaches	dances

Read the sentences in Activity 5 out loud. Practice saying the verb endings.

7 Write Write two sentences next to each picture. What are their jobs? What do they do every day?

1. _____

_____

2. _____

_____

3. _____

_____

4. _____

_____

8 Group Practice Work with a large group or with the whole class.

A. Write the name of a job on a sheet of paper. Then write what that person does every day. Pretend it is your job.

B. Ask other students what they do. Ask what they do every day. Write your classmates' names and jobs.

NAME	JOB	WHAT HE OR SHE DOES EVERY DAY
José	mechanic	He fixes cars.

1 Read and Listen Read the story. Listen to the story.

Two Neighborhoods

Ping and Tanya live in different neighborhoods, but they go to the same school. Tanya walks to school. The school is right across the street from her apartment building. Ping drives to school. She lives about fifteen minutes from the school.

Tanya lives in an apartment in a very busy neighborhood. There is a park across the street from her apartment building, right behind the school. There are a lot of stores and businesses in Tanya's neighborhood. There is a post office, and there are several restaurants nearby. There is a movie theater on the next block, and there is a supermarket and drugstore near the movie theater. There is a nice café right next to her apartment building.

Ping doesn't live in an apartment. She lives in a house. There are no big buildings in Ping's neighborhood. There aren't any restaurants. There is a small grocery store a few blocks away, but there aren't any supermarkets near her home. Her neighborhood is very quiet. There is a bank one block away. But most of the buildings in Ping's neighborhood are small private homes. It isn't very busy. That's the kind of neighborhood Ping likes to live in.

2 Write How are Ping's and Tanya's neighborhoods different? Complete the sentences.

1. Tanya _____ to school. Ping _____ to school.

2. Tanya lives in an _____ . Ping lives in a _____ .

3. There _____ a lot of stores in Tanya's neighborhood.

4. There _____ any restaurants in Ping's neighborhood.

5. Ping's neighborhood is very _____ . It isn't very _____ .

3 **Listen** Listen and write the names of the places on the map.

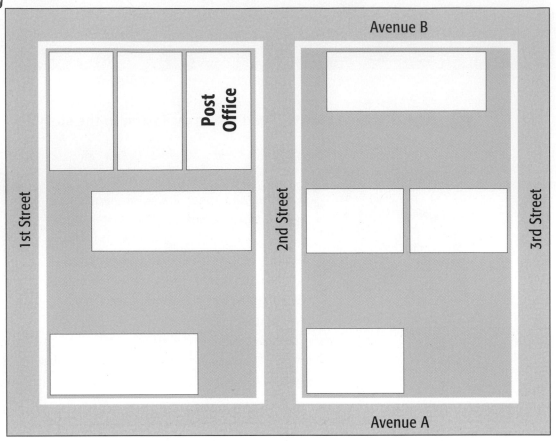

4 **Write** Look at the map and answer the questions.

1. Where is the post office? _____

   _____

2. Where is the bank? _____

   _____

3. Where is the library? _____

   _____

4. I am at the drugstore. How can I get to the clinic? _____

   _____

5. I am at the clinic. How can I get to the supermarket? _____

   _____

5 Best Answer Bubble the correct answers.

<table>
<tr><td></td><td>a</td><td>b</td><td>c</td></tr>
</table>

1. You can fill a prescription at the _____ .
   a) bookstore   b) library   c) drugstore ○ ○ ○

2. You can wash your clothes at the _____ .
   a) gas station   b) laundromat   c) car wash ○ ○ ○

3. She works in a restaurant. She's a _____ .
   a) hair stylist   b) server   c) receptionist ○ ○ ○

4. What do mechanics do? They _____ cars.
   a) fix   b) fixes   c) are fixing ○ ○ ○

5. He's getting a flu shot. He's at the _____ .
   a) florist   b) clinic   c) beauty salon ○ ○ ○

6. She _____ English every day.
   a) teach   b) teaching   c) teaches ○ ○ ○

6 Write Correct the mistakes in the sentences. If there are no mistakes, write *correct*.

1. I'm going to the post office. I'm need to mail a letter.

   _____

2. Going to the corner and turning right. The bank is on the left.

   _____

3. A salesperson sell things.

   _____

4. A mechanic fixs cars.

   _____

5. There are several restaurants in my neighborhood.

   _____

6. I'm going to the supermarket. I need a groceries.

   _____

7 Pronunciation Listen to the ending sounds of the verbs. Write the verbs in the correct column.

/s/	/z/	/iz/
_____	_____	_____
_____	_____	_____
_____	_____	_____

8 Teamwork Task Work in a team of three or four students. Work together to create your ideal neighborhood. Write eight places you want in your neighborhood on the map.

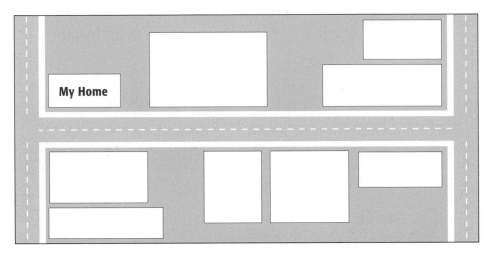

My Home

I can . . .			
• identify places in the community.	1	2	3
• describe locations.	1	2	3
• ask for and give directions.	1	2	3
• identify service agencies in the community.	1	2	3
• identify postal services.	1	2	3
• identify banking services.	1	2	3
• fill out a bank deposit slip.	1	2	3
• read destination signs on buses.	1	2	3
• write about my neighborhood.	1	2	3
• compare two neighborhoods.	1	2	3
• identify jobs and workplaces in the community.	1	2	3
• describe job duties.	1	2	3
• talk about habitual activities.	1	2	3

1 = not well   2 = OK   3 = very well

DOWNTOWN

9 **Write** Write the missing words in the story. Use these words: *is, are, isn't, café, park, quiet, left, straight, on, drive.*

Tanya: I love my new neighborhood. There (1) _____ so many nice places nearby.

Ping: What kind of places?
Tanya: There (2) _____ a wonderful (3) _____ right here behind us.

Tanya: There's a movie theater (4) _____ up 3rd Street on the (5) _____ .
Ping: There (6) _____ a movie theater in my neighborhood.

Tanya: There's a nice little (7) _____ where I can go to relax or exercise.
Ping: I (8) _____ to the gym to exercise every day.

Tanya: There's a big supermarket (9) _____ 3rd Street. And the school is right across from my apartment.
Ping: The school is pretty far from my house.

Ping: But my neighborhood is very (10) _____ and safe. That's really important to me.
Tanya: Then we both have the kind of neighborhoods we want!

10 **Pair Practice** Work with a partner. Practice the conversation. Student 1 is Tanya. Student 2 is Ping.

Health and Safety

GOALS

- ✓ Identify parts of the body.
- ✓ Ask about and tell health problems.
- ✓ Express sympathy.
- ✓ Describe symptoms.
- ✓ Read a medical appointment card.
- ✓ Take phone messages.
- ✓ Make a medical appointment.
- ✓ Follow directions during a medical exam.
- ✓ Write an absence note.
- ✓ Recommend over-the-counter medicines.
- ✓ Call in sick.
- ✓ Call 911 to report an emergency.
- ✓ Read and respond to safety signs.
- ✓ Read medicine labels.

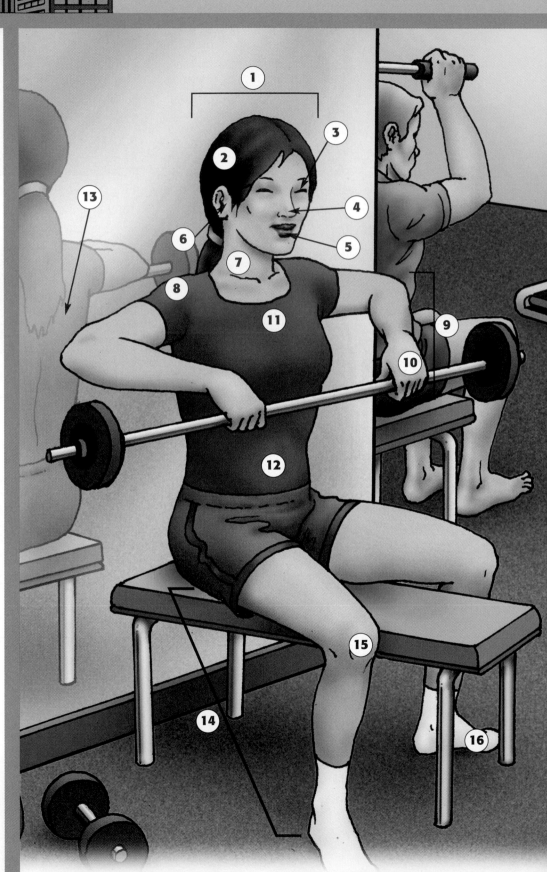

1. head
2. hair
3. eyes
4. nose
5. mouth
6. ears
7. neck
8. shoulder
9. arm
10. hand
11. chest
12. stomach
13. back
14. leg
15. knee
16. foot

② **Pronunciation**

• shoulder

• stomach

1 **Say It** Listen to the conversation. Say it with a partner.

head

A: What's the matter?
B: My <u>head</u> hurts.
A: Oh, I'm sorry to hear that.

Practice more conversations. Use the pictures below.

1. arm

2. foot

3. back

4. shoulder

5. ear

6. knee

Word Help: Irregular plurals

Most plural nouns end in -s, but some nouns have irregular plurals.

Singular	Plural	Singular	Plural
man	men	foot	feet
woman	women	tooth	teeth
child	children	mouse	mice
person	people		

2 **Write** Complete the sentences with the singular or plural form.

1. (foot)   Those two men have problems with their ____feet____ .

2. (tooth)   It's important to brush your _____ every morning.

3. (person)   She is the smartest _____ I know.

4. (mouse)   _____ in the kitchen can cause health problems.

5. (person)   Many _____ take aspirin for headaches.

6. (foot)   My left _____ has six toes.

7. (child)   All _____ should go to school.

8. (man / woman) All _____ and _____ should see a doctor regularly.

3 **Listen** Listen and write the parts of the body. Some are singular and some are plural.

1. _____

2. _____

3. _____

4. _____

5. _____

6. _____

7. _____

8. _____

9. _____

10. _____

4 **Say It** Listen to the conversation. Say it with a partner.

A: How are you today?

B: Not so good.

A: What's the matter?

B: My head hurts. And I have a <u>sore throat</u>, too.

sore throat

Practice more conversations. Use the pictures below.

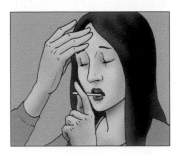

1. fever

2. runny nose

3. bad cough

GRAMMAR CHECK

Verb or adjective?

Sometimes we use a verb (*hurt*) to talk about medical problems.
    My foot **hurts**.
Sometimes we use an adjective (*sore*) to talk about the problem.
    I have a **sore** foot.

5 **Write** Rewrite the sentences. Change the verbs to adjectives. Change the adjectives to verbs.

1. My foot hurts.   I have a _____*sore*_____ foot.

2. My toe hurts.   _____

3. My knee hurts.   _____

4. My shoulder hurts.   _____

5. _____   I have a sore throat.

6. _____   I have a sore finger.

7. _____   I have a sore leg.

Word Help: More health problems

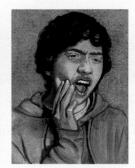

a headache   a stomachache   a backache   a toothache   an earache

6 Pronunciation Listen and repeat the words. Stress the first syllable.

headache   stomachache   backache

toothache   earache

7 Group Practice Work with a large group or the whole class.

A. Choose a medical problem from this lesson. Pretend you have this problem.

B. Ask your classmates how they are today. Find a classmate with the same problem as you.

C. Tell your teacher the problem.

Example: I have a headache and Rosa has a headache, too.

Game Time

Teacher says

Work with a large group or the whole class. Stand up. Listen to your teacher. When your teacher says, "Teacher says, touch your nose," you touch your nose. When your teacher says, "Touch your nose," (but not *Teacher says*) you don't touch your nose. If you make a mistake, sit down.

The Doctor's Office

Lesson 2

1 🎧 **Say It** Listen to the conversation. Say it with a partner.

> Dr. Martinez
> APPOINTMENT CARD
> Your appointment is
> Mon. 4/15, 11:00 A.M.
> in
> Room 205

A: When is your appointment with Doctor Martinez?
B: It's on <u>Monday, April 15th</u>.
A: What time?
B: It's at <u>eleven o'clock</u>.
A: What room is it in?
B: It's in <u>Room 205</u>.

Practice more conversations. Use the pictures below.

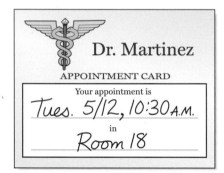

> Dr. Martinez
> APPOINTMENT CARD
> Your appointment is
> Tues. 5/12, 10:30 A.M.
> in
> Room 18

1.

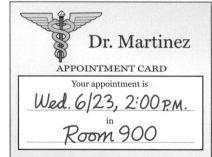

> Dr. Martinez
> APPOINTMENT CARD
> Your appointment is
> Wed. 6/23, 2:00 P.M.
> in
> Room 900

2.

2 🎧 **Listen** Listen to the telephone messages. Write the date, time, and place of the appointment.

> DR. JOHNSON, MD.
> DATE:
> TIME:
> ROOM:

1.

> BAYSIDE MEDICAL GROUP
> Date:
> Time:
> Room:

2.

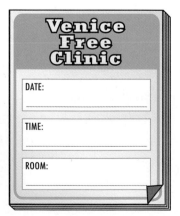

> Venice Free Clinic
> DATE:
> TIME:
> ROOM:

3.

3 **Say It** Listen to the conversation. Say it with a partner.

A: My <u>daughter</u> has <u>a headache</u>. What do you recommend for <u>a headache</u>?

B: Give <u>her</u> some <u>aspirin</u>. <u>Aspirin</u> is good for <u>a headache</u>.

daughter / a headache

Practice more conversations. Use the pictures below.

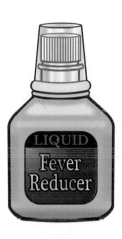

1. **son / a bad cough**

2. **wife / a fever**

3. **father / a sore throat**

GRAMMAR CHECK

Object pronouns	
Subject pronoun	*Object pronoun*
He	Him
She	Her
She has a headache. (subject)	Give **her** some aspirin. (object)

4 **Write** Complete the sentences with an object pronoun.

1. My daughter has a toothache.   Take _____ to a dentist.

2. My son has a high fever.   Take _____ to a pediatrician.

3. My wife is pregnant.   Take _____ to an OB/GYN.

4. My brother feels sad all the time.   Take _____ to a psychologist.

5 **Say It** Listen to the conversation. Say it with a partner.

A: I want to make an appointment for my <u>son</u>. <u>He</u> has <u>a bad headache</u>.

B: Does <u>he</u> have a fever, too?

A: Yes, <u>he</u> does. He has a <u>103°</u> temperature.

B: Can you bring <u>him</u> in at three o'clock?

A: Yes, I can.

son / a bad headache

Practice more conversations. Use the pictures below.

1. daughter / a bad stomachache

2. grandson / the flu

Word Help: Body Temperature

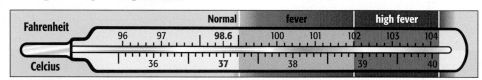

			Normal		fever		high fever	
Fahrenheit	96	97	98.6	100	101	102	103	104
Celcius		36	37	38		39		40

GRAMMAR CHECK

Short answers

Short answers use the same helping verb as the question.

Example: **Do** you have a headache?   Yes, I **do**.   No, I **don't**. (do not)

Can you speak English?   Yes, I **can**.   No, I **can't**. (can not)

6 **Write** Complete the sentences with *do, does,* or *can*—positive or negative.

1. Do you have a headache? Yes, I _____ .

2. Can you come in tomorrow? Yes, I _____ .

3. Does your son have a sore throat? Yes, he _____ .

4. Do you have a fever? No, I _____ .

5. Can you bring him in today? No, I _____ .

6. Does she have a fever, too? No, she _____ .

7 **Pair Practice** Work with a partner. You are a doctor and patient.
Doctor: Read the sentences.
Patient: Do the actions.

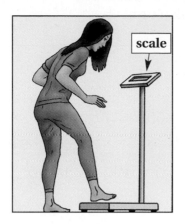

1. Please step on the scale.

2. Please sit on the examination table.

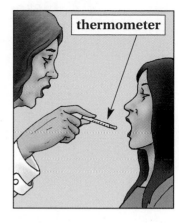

3. Put the thermometer under your tongue.

4. Open your mouth and say, "Aaahh."

5. Take a deep breath.

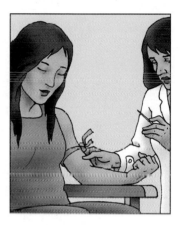

6. Hold out your arm and make a fist.

GRAMMAR CHECK

Imperative *vs.* present continuous

Use imperatives for commands or directions.
Step on the scale. Please **sit** on the examination table.

Use the present continuous to tell what someone is doing now.
She **is stepping** on the scale.

8 **Write** Look at the pictures in Activity 7. Write what Ping is doing in each picture.

9 **Listen** Listen and write the missing words.

> November 15
> Dear Ms. Ryan:
>   I ____ writing ____ note for my son, Victor Alvarez. ____ is absent from school today because he is sick. He ____ a headache and a ____.
> I think he has the flu. I hope he will be back ____ school ____ Monday.
> Sincerely,
> *Norma Alvarez*

10 **Write** Use the note to answer the questions.

1. Who is writing the note? _____

2. Who is sick? _____

3. What are his symptoms? _____

4. What illness does Victor probably have? _____

5. When will he be back in school? _____

6. Who is Victor's teacher? _____

11 **Teamwork Task** Work in teams of three or four. Work together to write an absence note for one person on your team. Write the date and your teacher's name. Tell the name of your teammate and what's wrong. Tell when he or she will be back in class.

Safety Rules

1 **Say It** Listen to the conversation. Say it with a partner.

A: Watch out!

B: What's wrong?

A: Don't <u>turn right</u> there.

B: Why not?

A: The sign says, <u>"No right turn."</u>

B: Oh. OK.

turn right

Practice more conversations. Use the pictures below.

1. park

2. smoke

3. turn around

4. go in

5. walk

6. use your cell phone

GRAMMAR CHECK

Negative commands or rules

Use *don't* or *do not* before the base form of a verb for negative commands.

Don't smoke here.

Do not use cell phones in class.

2 Say It Listen to the conversation. Say it with a partner.

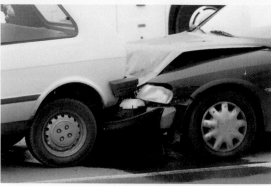
a car accident

A: Emergency Operator, 911.

B: Hello, this is (*your name*). I want to report an emergency.

A: What is the emergency?

B: It's <u>a car accident</u>.

A: What is the location?

B: Main Street and Avenue B in Santa Monica.

A: OK. An ambulance is on the way.

Practice more conversations. Use the pictures below.

1. a fire

2. a heart attack

Note: The ambulance is *on the way* = The ambulance is coming now.

3 Write Read the problems. Write "Call 911" for the emergencies. Write "Don't call 911" for the problems that are not emergencies.

1. A man is stealing a car. _____

2. There is a car accident. _____

3. A man is running in the street. _____

4. Some teenagers are fighting in the street. _____

5. A woman is having a baby in the street. _____

6. My teacher is late for class. _____

4 **Say It** Listen to the conversation. Say it with a partner.

Tanya / the flu

A: Hello. This is <u>Tanya</u>.

B: Hello, <u>Tanya</u>. How are you?

A: Not so good. I can't come to work today.

B: What's the matter?

A: I'm sick. I have <u>the flu</u>.

B: OK. I hope you feel better soon.

A: Thank you.

Practice more conversations. Use the pictures below.

1. Ping / a high fever

2. Jenny / a really bad headache

3. Marco / a bad stomachache

Culture Tip

Call in sick

Don't go to work if you are really sick. Go to work if you have only a cold or you are just a little sick. Always call in sick if you can't go to work. Also, call if you are late.

5 **Write** What are reasons to stay home from work? Check (✓) the good reasons and the bad reasons.

	GOOD REASON	BAD REASON
1. I'm tired.	_____	_____
2. I have a broken leg.	_____	_____
3. I had a serious car accident.	_____	_____
4. I have a runny nose.	_____	_____
5. I have a sore knee.	_____	_____
6. I have a 103 degree temperature.	_____	_____
7. I have a cough.	_____	_____

Write more good and bad reasons.

6 **Write** Read the medicine labels. Circle *true* or *false*.

Medicine A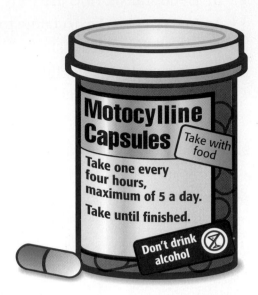

Medicine B

1. You can drive after taking Medicine A.   True   False
2. Medicine B is safe for children.   True   False
3. You can drink wine with these medicines.   True   False
4. Take Medicine A with your dinner.   True   False
5. You can take five capsules of Medicine A in one day.   True   False
6. You can take five tablets of Medicine B in one day.   True   False

7 **Teamwork Task** Work in teams of three or four. Write rules for your class or school. Use *don't* or *do not*.

Example: Don't smoke in class.

_____

_____

_____

_____

_____

_____

1 **Read and Listen** Read the story. Listen to the story.

Sick

"Hi, Jenny," Ping says. "Are you OK? You don't look so good."

"I don't know," Jenny says. "I think I'm sick."

"What's the matter?"

"I have a headache and body aches."

"Where does it hurt?"

"My whole body hurts. My legs hurt. My back hurts. My chest hurts. Even my hair hurts."

"Your hair hurts?"

"No, my hair doesn't really hurt. But everything else hurts and I'm tired all the time."

"Do you have a fever?" Ping puts her hand on Jenny's forehead. It feels hot. "I think you have a fever," Ping says. "You need to see a doctor. You probably have the flu."

"How about you? Do you feel OK?"

"No, I don't. I'm tired all the time, too, and I have a stomachache."

"That's terrible. Maybe we both need to go home and rest."

"Good idea. Tomorrow we both need to see a doctor."

2 **Write** Circle *true* or *false*.

1. Jenny and Ping are both sick.	True	False
2. Jenny has a headache.	True	False
3. Ping has a headache.	True	False
4. Jenny's hair hurts.	True	False
5. Jenny probably has a fever.	True	False
6. Jenny and Ping are both tired.	True	False

❸ Pair Practice Work with a partner. Practice the conversation in Activity 1.

❹ Write Write the parts of the body.

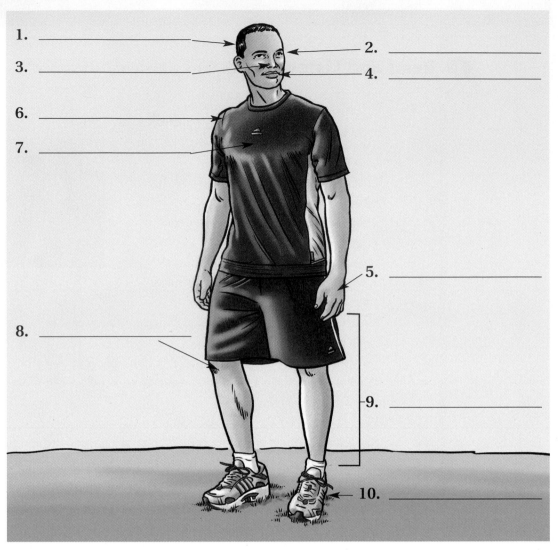

1. _____

2. _____

3. _____

4. _____

6. _____

7. _____

5. _____

8. _____

9. _____

10. _____

❺ Listen Listen and write the sentences.

1. _____

2. _____

3. _____

4. _____

5. _____

6. _____

6 **Best Answer** Bubble the correct answers.

a   b   c

1. Both of my _____ hurt.
   a) foot   b) foots   c) feet   ○ ○ ○

2. I have a _____ back.
   a) sore   b) pain   c) hurts   ○ ○ ○

3. The _____ is below the stomach.
   a) shoulder   b) chest   c) knee   ○ ○ ○

4. Go to the doctor. You probably have _____ .
   a) a pain   b) the flu   c) an aspirin   ○ ○ ○

5. Please, stand up. I am _____ up.
   a) stand   b) standing   c) stood   ○ ○ ○

6. Please put the _____ in your mouth.
   a) scale   b) stethoscope   c) thermometer   ○ ○ ○

7 **Write** Correct the mistakes in the sentences. If there are no mistakes, write *correct*.

1. My head hurt. I have a headache.

   _____

2. I need to go to the dentist. I have a teethache.

   _____

3. I have a very sore foot.

   _____

4. Take your temperature to see if you have an earache.

   _____

5. Not go in there. The sign says, "Do not enter."

   _____

6. She has a cold. She has a cough and she has a running nose.

   _____

8 **Pronunciation** Listen and repeat the singular and plural forms of the words.

man	men	foot	feet
woman	women	tooth	teeth
child	children	mouse	mice

9 Listen Listen and circle the word you hear.

1. man   men
2. foot   feet
3. woman   women
4. tooth   teeth
5. child   children
6. mouse   mice

10 Teamwork Task Work in teams of four. Choose the job you want.
Student 1 is the artist.
Students 2 and 3 are the teachers.
Student 4 is the writer.

Student 1: Get a large piece of paper and draw a picture of a person. It can be a man, woman, or child.

Students 2 and 3: Look at the picture. Point at parts of the body and name them.

Student 4: Write the names of the parts of the body on the picture. Only write the words your teammates tell you.

I can . . .			
• identify parts of the body.	1	2	3
• ask about and tell health problems.	1	2	3
• express sympathy.	1	2	3
• describe symptoms.	1	2	3
• read a medical appointment card.	1	2	3
• take phone messages.	1	2	3
• make a medical appointment.	1	2	3
• follow directions during a medical exam.	1	2	3
• write an absence note.	1	2	3
• recommend over-the-counter medicines.	1	2	3
• call in sick.	1	2	3
• call 911 to report an emergency.	1	2	3
• read and respond to safety signs.	1	2	3
• read medicine labels.	1	2	3

1 = not well   2 = OK   3 = very well

DOWNTOWN

11 **Write** Write the missing words in the story. Use these words: *do, symptoms, scale, blood pressure, fever, temperature, healthy, stomachache, appointment, take.*

Receptionist: Do you have an
(1) _____ with Dr. Martinez?
Ping: Yes, I (2) _____ . It's at three o'clock.

Nurse: Do you have any (3) _____ ?
Ping: I'm really tired and I have a
(4) _____ .

Nurse: Please step on the (5) _____ .
Do you have a (6) _____ ? Let's check
your (7) _____ .

Nurse: Your temperature is normal.
Let's check your (8) _____ , and
(9) _____ some blood.

Doctor: Well, Ping, you aren't sick.
In fact, you are very (10) _____ .
Ping: That's good.
Doctor: But you are pregnant.

Ping: I'm pregnant?
Doctor: Yes, you are. Congratulations!
Ping: Wow! I need to call my husband
right now!

12 **Pair Practice** Work with three partners. Practice the conversation.
Student 1 is the receptionist. Student 2 is Ping. Student 3 is the nurse.
Student 4 is the doctor.

Work

162

1 **Listen** *Listen and repeat the sentences.*

1. He is an auto mechanic.
   He fixes cars.

2. She is a hair stylist.
   She cuts and styles hair.

3. He is a house painter.
   He paints houses.

4. She is a salesperson.
   She sells clothes.

1 **Say It** Listen to the conversation. Say it with a partner.

A: What's <u>Julia</u> doing?

B: <u>She's</u> <u>cutting hair</u>.

A: Why is <u>she</u> <u>cutting hair</u>?

B: It's <u>her</u> job. <u>She</u> <u>cuts hair</u> every day at work.

Julia / cutting hair

Practice more conversations. Use the pictures below.

1. Alison / teaching English

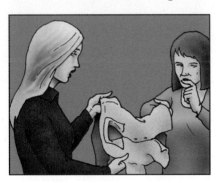

2. Tanya / selling clothes

3. Marco / cooking food

2 **Match** Match to complete the sentences.

_____ 1. A salesperson . . .   **a.** drives a taxi.

_____ 2. A house painter . . .   **b.** takes care of children.

_____ 3. A doctor . . .   **c.** fixes things.

_____ 4. A pharmacist . . .   **d.** sells things.

_____ 5. A repair person . . .   **e.** paints houses.

_____ 6. A child care worker . . .   **f.** delivers things.

_____ 7. A taxi driver . . .   **g.** fills prescriptions.

_____ 8. A delivery person . . .   **h.** helps sick people.

3 **Write** Close your books. On a sheet of paper write five sentences from Activity 2.

4 **Say It** Listen to the conversation. Say it with a partner.

house painter / paints houses

A: What does he do?
B: He's a <u>house painter</u>. He <u>paints houses</u>.
A: Is he working now?
B: Yes. He's <u>painting a house</u> right now.

Practice more conversations. Use the pictures below.

1. truck driver / drives trucks

2. pizza delivery person / delivers pizzas

3. computer assembler / assembles computers

5 **Write** Read the job duties. Write sentences about what the workers are doing now.

JOB DUTIES	WHAT ARE THEY DOING RIGHT NOW?
1. He fixes cars.	<u>He is fixing a car right now.</u>
2. She delivers pizzas.	
3. She makes dresses.	
4. He cleans houses.	
5. She takes care of children.	
6. He sells computers.	
7. He drives a taxi.	
8. She helps doctors.	

can/can't

Use *can* to show that someone is able to do something.
   I **can** ride a bicycle.
Use *can't* to show that someone is not able to do something.
   I **can** ride a bicycle, but my grandmother **can't** ride a bicycle.

Subject	can/can't	Base verb	
I/You	can		
He/She/It	can not (can't)	ride	a bicycle.
We/They			

Check Point:
✓ We usually use the contraction *can't* for the negative form.
   I **can't** ride a bicycle.

6 **Say It** Listen to the conversation. Say it with a partner.

make clothes / seamstress

A: What job skills do you have?

B: Job skills?

A: Yes, what can you do?

B: I can <u>make clothes</u>. I was <u>a seamstress</u> in my country.

A: That's a good job skill.

Practice more conversations. Use the pictures below.

1. **drive a taxi /
   taxi driver**

2. **make cabinets /
   carpenter**

3. **use a computer /
   office assistant**

4. **file / file clerk**

5. **teach children /
   teacher**

6. **manage people /
   manager**

7 Pair Practice Work with a partner. Ask your partner if he or she can do any of the job skills in Activity 6.

Example: *Student 1:* Can you make clothes?
Student 2: Yes, I can. *OR* No, I can't.

8 Pronunciation Listen and repeat the sentences.

When we use *can*, we stress the verb after *can*. We don't stress *can*.
I can **cook** Chinese food.
She can **type** very well.
He can **fix** cars.

When we use *can't*, we stress *can't* more than the verb.
He **can't** cook.
I **can't** type very well.
She **can't** fix cars.

9 Write Write about your partner's job skills. Use the skills in Activity 6. Use *can* or *can't*.

Example: Carlos can't make clothes.

Tell your teacher about your partner's job skills.

10 Group Practice Work with a large group or the whole class. Find someone who can do the skills below. Write one classmate's name on each line.

Example: *Student 1:* Can you drive a truck?
Student 2: Yes, I can. *OR* No, I can't.

1. _____ can drive a truck.

2. _____ can ride a bicycle.

3. _____ can use a computer.

4. _____ can take care of children.

5. _____ can paint houses.

Game Time

Your teacher will write a job skill on a piece of paper. Try to guess what it is.
Example: *Student 1:* Can you fix cars?   *Teacher:* No, I can't.
           Student 2: Can you cook well?   *Teacher:* Yes, I can.

Help Wanted

1 **Say It** Listen to the conversation. Say it with a partner.

HELP WANTED
Office Assistant
Type thirty words per minute.
Call (818) 555-3132.

A: Hello. I'm calling about the office assistant position.

B: Yes. Can you type thirty words per minute?

A: Yes, I can.

B: Great. Can you come in tomorrow for an interview?

A: Yes, I can.

Practice more conversations. Use the job ads below.

Driver Wanted
Drive a truck.
$15/hr.
Call (818) 555-2591.

COOK WANTED
Cook Chinese food.
$12/hr.
Call (818) 555-8792.

Baby Sitter Wanted
Take care of small children.
$10/hr.
Call (818) 555-3443.

Word Help: *can*
Use *can* with the base verb.
Don't add *-s* to the verb for *he, she*, or *it* when you use *can*.
    She **cooks** every day.   She **can** cook.

---

2 **Write** Write the sentences about job duties and skills.

JOB DUTIES	JOB SKILLS
1. He fixes cars at work.	He can fix cars.
2. She uses a computer at work.	_____
3. He manages people at work.	_____
4. I teach English at work.	_____
5. _____	He can drive and park cars.
6. _____	They can sell computers.
7. _____	She can take care of children.
8. _____	I can deliver letters and packages.

3 Read Read the "Help Wanted" ads. <u>Underline</u> the job titles. (Circle) the abbreviations.

Help Wanted

PT Cashier, eves & wknds.
Bilingual–Spanish/English.
Must have 6 mo. exp. $10/hr.

1.

Help Wanted

FT Office Asst.
M–F, 10–6.
Must type, ans. phones and
take messages.
No exp. nec. $12/hr.
Call for appt. (818) 555-3233.

2.

4 Match Match the abbreviations in the ads with the words below.

1. part time	PT	7. necessary	_____
2. full time	_____	8. appointment	_____
3. evenings	_____	9. Monday to Friday	_____
4. months	_____	10. assistant	_____
5. hour	_____	11. answer	_____
6. weekends	_____	12. experience	_____

5 Write Answer the questions about the jobs in Activity 3.

1. Which job is full time? _____

2. Which job requires typing skills? _____

3. Which job requires work on Saturday? _____

4. Which job pays $12 per hour? _____

5. Which job requires experience? _____

6. Which job requires two languages? _____

7. Which job is available right now? _____

8. Which job do I have to call for an appointment? _____

Say It Listen to the conversation. Say it with a partner.

CASHIER WANTED
$10/hr.
Must work nights.
Call (818) 555-8390.

A: Here's a job for a <u>cashier</u>.

B: What does it say?

A: It says <u>ten dollars per hour</u>.

B: What else?

A: It says "<u>must work nights</u>." Can you <u>work nights</u>?

B: Yes, I can.

A: Great. You can apply for the job.

Practice more conversations. Use the "Help Wanted" ads below.

Help Wanted Office Assistant
FT. Good pay.
Must speak Chinese and English.
Call for appt. (818) 555-0032.

1.

HELP WANTED
Preschool Child Care Worker
$10/hr. Must work with small children.
CALL (818) 555-9901.

2.

HELP WANTED
DELIVERY DRIVER
Excellent pay.
Must drive a small truck.
Call (818) 555-2111.

3.

Word Help: *must / have to*
Use *must* or *have to* to show that something is necessary.
It is necessary to work nights. = You **must** work nights. = You **have to** work nights.
Must is formal. *Have to* is informal or personal.

7 **Say It** Listen to the conversation. Say it with a partner.

A: I'm calling about the job for an <u>office assistant</u>. Can you tell me about the job?

B: Yes, the pay is <u>$14</u> per hour and you <u>must type forty words per minute</u>.

A: Oh.

B: Can you <u>type forty words per minute</u>?

A: No, I can't.

B: I'm sorry. You have to <u>type forty words per minute</u> for this job.

Practice more conversations. Use the "Help Wanted" ads below.

1.

2.

3.

Note: Skills

A skill is something you have to learn how to do. Not everyone can do it.
Playing the guitar is a skill. Only some people can do it.
Listening to music is not a skill. Anyone can do it.
Skills that you can use on a job are **job skills**.

8 **Teamwork Task** Work in teams of four. Ask your teammates about their skills. Write their skills in the chart.

NAME	JOB SKILLS	OTHER SKILLS

Job Applications

Lesson 3

1 **Say It** Listen to the conversation. Say it with a partner.

JOB APPLICATION		
NAME *Ryan, Alison*		
WORK HISTORY		
Dates	Position	Employer
2005-Present	English Teacher	Los Angeles Adult School
2003–2005	Teacher Assistant	Santa Monica Adult School

A: What is <u>Alison's</u> current job?

B: <u>She</u> is <u>an English teacher</u>.

A: What was <u>her</u> previous job?

B: <u>She</u> was <u>a teacher assistant</u>.

A: When was <u>she</u> <u>a teacher assistant</u>?

B: <u>She</u> was <u>a teacher assistant</u> <u>from 2003 to 2005</u>.

Practice more conversations. Use the job applications below.

JOB APPLICATION		
NAME Garcia, Carlos		
WORK HISTORY		
Dates	Position	Employer
2007-Present	Mechanic	Honest Auto Repair
2005–2007	Mechanic's Helper	Ventura Auto

1.

JOB APPLICATION		
NAME Lopez, Marco		
WORK HISTORY		
Dates	Position	Employer
1/06-Present	Cook	The Downtown Café
1/05 – 1/06	Kitchen Helper	The Old Town Café

2.

Word Help: Job history
Your *current job* is the job you have now.
Your *previous jobs* are the jobs you had in the past.

to be

Subject	Present be		Subject	Past be	
I	**am**	a teacher.	I	**was**	a student.
He/She	**is**	a teacher.	He/She	**was**	a student.
We	**are**	teachers.	We	**were**	students.
You	**are**	a teacher.	You	**were**	a student.
They	**are**	teachers.	They	**were**	students.

2 Write Answer the questions with complete sentences.

1. What is Marco's current job? _____

2. What was Marco's previous job? _____

3. What is your current job? _____

4. What was your previous job? _____

5. What is/was your father's job? _____

6. What is/was your mother's job? _____

7. What was your grandfather's job? _____

3 Pair Practice Work with a partner. Ask and answer the questions in Activity 2.

4 Listen Listen and write the sentences. Listen for present or past tense verbs.

1. _____

2. _____

3. _____

4. _____

5. _____

6. _____

5 Group Practice Work with a large group or with the whole class. Ask four classmates about their current and previous jobs. Write in the chart.

NAME	CURRENT JOB	PREVIOUS JOB

6 Say It Listen to the conversation. Say it with a partner.

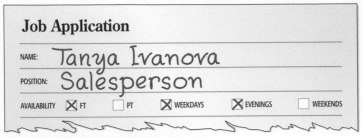

Job Application

NAME: Tanya Ivanova
POSITION: Salesperson
AVAILABILITY ☒ FT ☐ PT ☒ WEEKDAYS ☒ EVENINGS ☐ WEEKENDS

A: What position is she applying for?

B: A <u>salesperson</u> position.

A: Does she want to work full time or part time?

B: She wants <u>full time</u>.

A: Can she work Monday to Friday?

B: <u>Yes, she can.</u>

A: Can she work evenings?

B: <u>Yes, she can.</u>

A: Can she work on Saturday and Sunday?

B: <u>No, she can't.</u>

Practice more conversations. Use the job applications below.

Job Application

NAME: Jenny Vidal
POSITION: Cashier
AVAILABILITY ☐ FT ☑ PT ☑ WEEKDAYS ☐ EVENINGS ☑ WEEKENDS

1.

Job Application

NAME: Monica Silva
POSITION: Teacher Assistant
AVAILABILITY ☐ FT ☒ PT ☒ WEEKDAYS ☒ EVENINGS ☐ WEEKENDS

2.

Culture Tip

Full time or part time?

In the United States, *full time* usually means thirty-five or forty hours a week. More than forty hours a week is *overtime*. Part time is less than thirty-five hours a week.

Short answers with *be*

Present tense	*Past tense*
Are you a teacher? Yes, **I am**. *OR* No, **I'm not**.	Were you a teacher in the past? Yes, **I was**. *OR* No, **I wasn't**.
Is he a teacher? Yes, **he is**. *OR* No, **he isn't**.	Was he a teacher in the past? Yes, **he was**. *OR* No, **he wasn't**.
Are they teachers? Yes, **they are**. *OR* No, **they aren't**.	Were they teachers in the past? Yes, **they were**. *OR* No, **they weren't**.

Check Point:

✓ We usually use contractions for short answers, but the complete form is also correct. Write the complete forms of the short answers.

I'm not. _____   He isn't. _____   They aren't. _____

I wasn't. _____   He wasn't. _____   They weren't. _____

7 **Pair Practice** Work with a partner. Ask and answer questions about now and the past.

Example: *Student 1:* Is he a teacher now?

Student 2: No, he isn't. He's a cashier.

Now

Now

Now

1. a teacher?   **2. a taxi driver?**   **3. cashiers?**

Past

Past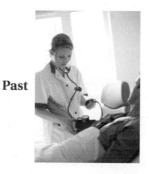

Past

Past

4. a mechanic?   **5. a receptionist?**   **6. nurses?**

8 Read Read the job application.

JOB APPLICATION

1. Position:	

2. Availability: ☐ Full-time ☐ Part-time ☐ Weekdays ☐ Weekends ☐ Evenings ☐ Weekends

PERSONAL INFORMATION

3. Name: Monica Silva

4. Address: 333 Lincoln Blvd., Venice, CA 90291

5. Tel: (310) _____   E-mail: _____

WORK HISTORY
(Start with current job)

	Dates	Position	Employer
6.	6/07-Present	Office Assistant	Jobs, Jobs, Jobs
7.		Teller	Bank of the West

EDUCATION

	Dates	School	Location
8.	1/07–6/08		Woodland Hills, CA 91367

SKILLS

9. _____ , all MS Office programs, bilingual: Portuguese, English

9 Write Where should Monica write the information? Write the line from the application.

1. 555-3253	Line	5
2. West Valley College	Line	___
3. Moca123@coldmail.com	Line	___
4. 1/05–6/07	Line	___
5. Teacher Assistant	Line	___
6. She wants a full-time job.	Line	___
7. She can type forty words per minute.	Line	___
8. She can work on weekends or weekdays.	Line	___

Now, write the missing information on Monica's job application.

10 Teamwork Task Work in teams of three or four. Use the information from the job application to write sentences about Monica. Work together to write as many sentences as you can on a sheet of paper.

Review

1 **Read and Listen** Read the story. Listen to the story.

New Jobs

Some of Ping's classmates are looking for new jobs. Jenny isn't happy with her current job. She is a cashier in a café, but in Colombia she was a manager of a café. She wants to be a manager again.

Julia isn't happy with her job, either. She works in a small beauty salon in a shopping mall. But she wants to work in a big expensive salon where she can make more money. She has good skills and experience. She can cut and style hair very well. She can also color hair. Right now, she is filling out an application for a job in Beverly Hills.

Han Do wants a new job, too. He is a house painter now, but he has good office skills. He can type, file, and answer phones. And he can manage people. He was an office manager in Vietnam. He wants to work in an office again. So, he is filling out an application for a job as an office assistant.

Ping doesn't want a new job now. She wants to learn some new skills and get a good job after her baby is born. Right now, she is just thinking about having a healthy baby.

2 **Write** Answer the questions.

1. Who is looking for a new job? _____

2. What was Jenny's job in Colombia? _____

3. Where does Julia want to work? _____

4. What job skills does Julia have? _____

5. What skills does Han Do have? _____

6. What was Han's job in Vietnam? _____

7. Who isn't looking for a job now? _____

8. What is Ping doing now? _____

3 **Write** Write four sentences under each picture. What are their jobs? What do they do at work? What are they doing now? What can they do?

1. He is a taxi driver.

   He drives a taxi.

   He is driving a taxi.

   He can drive a taxi.

2. _____

   _____

   _____

   _____

3. _____

   _____

   _____

   _____

4. I am a . . . _____

   _____

   _____

   _____

4 **Listen** Listen and write the sentences.

1. _____

2. _____

3. _____

4. _____

5. _____

5 **Best Answer** Bubble the correct answers.

   a   b   c

1. A hair stylist works in a _____ .   ○ ○ ○
   a) hospital   **b)** clothing store   **c)** beauty salon

2. She's working now. She's _____ a taxi.   ○ ○ ○
   a) driver   **b)** driving   **c)** drive

3. _____ she drive a truck?   ○ ○ ○
   a) Is   **b)** Can   **c)** Do

4. She _____ a nurse in her previous job.   ○ ○ ○
   a) was   **b)** can   **c)** is

5. They _____ nurses in their last job.   ○ ○ ○
   a) are   **b)** can   **c)** were

6 **Write** Correct the mistakes in the sentences. If there are no mistakes, write *correct*.

1. A delivery person deliver things. _____

2. House painters can paint houses. _____

3. A bilingual person can speaks two languages. _____

4. In his previous job, he is a teacher. _____

5. What job can you applying for now? _____

6. Can she fix cars? Yes, she is. _____

7 **Pair Practice** Work with a partner. Look at the "Help Wanted" ad. Ask and answer questions about the job.

★ **HELP WANTED** ★
Cashier
PT, eves and wknds.
Must have 6 mo. exp. $12/hr.
Call (818) 555-6002.

8 **Pronunciation** Listen and circle the word you hear.

1. can   can't   5. can   can't
2. can   can't   6. can   can't
3. can   can't   7. can   can't
4. can   can't   8. can   can't

9 **Teamwork Task** Work in teams of five. Work together to fill out the job application for the volunteer.

Student 1 is the volunteer.
Student 2: Ask the volunteer about the job he or she wants and when he or she can work.
Student 3: Ask about the volunteer's personal information.
Student 4: Ask about the volunteer's work history.
Student 5: Ask about the volunteer's education and skills.

JOB APPLICATION

1. Position: _____

2. Availability: ☐ Full-time ☐ Part-time ☐ Weekdays ☐ Weekends ☐ Evenings ☐ Weekends

PERSONAL INFORMATION

3. Name: _____

4. Address: _____

5. Tel: _____ E-mail: _____

WORK HISTORY *(Start with current job)*	Dates	Position	Employer
6.			
7.			

EDUCATION	Dates	School	Location
8.			

SKILLS	
9.	

I can . . .

• identify common occupations.	1	2	3
• talk about job duties.	1	2	3
• contrast simple present and present continuous.	1	2	3
• talk about job skills.	1	2	3
• write about job skills.	1	2	3
• read "Help Wanted" ads.	1	2	3
• respond to "Help Wanted" ads.	1	2	3
• talk about work history.	1	2	3
• use was/were for past jobs.	1	2	3
• describe availability for work.	1	2	3
• fill out a job application.	1	2	3

1 = not well   2 = OK   3 = very well

DOWNTOWN

10 **Write** Write the missing words in the story. Use these words: *office, "Help Wanted", painter, paint, was, wasn't, skills, must, application, can.*

Ping: Hello, Han. What are you doing?
Han: I'm filling out a job (1) _____ .

Ping: What job are you applying for?
Han: It's an (2) _____ assistant position working in a small office.

Ping: But aren't you a house (3) _____ ?
Han: Right now I (4) _____ houses. But I (5) _____ a house painter in my country. I (6) _____ an office manager.

Ping: Do you have good office (7) _____ ?
Han: Yes, I do. I (8) _____ use a computer and type very well.

Han: Unfortunately, it says one more thing in the (9) _____ ad.
Ping: What does it say?
Han: It says you (10) _____ have good English skills.

Ping: Well, don't worry. Pretty soon you will have very good English skills.
Han: I hope so, Ping. I really hope so.

11 **Pair Practice** Work with a partner. Practice the conversation. Student 1 is Ping. Student 2 is Han.

Future Plans

CONGRATULATIONS!

182

GOALS

✓ Identify foods and food groups.

✓ Talk about future plans.

✓ Talk about likes and dislikes.

✓ Identify *dos* and *don'ts* for a job interview.

✓ Understand U.S. workplace expectations.

✓ Read a work schedule.

✓ Understand a pay stub.

✓ Interpret a W2 form.

✓ Use personality adjectives at a job interview.

✓ Understand an employee evaluation form.

✓ Complete an employee evaluation form.

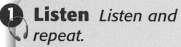

1. Listen *Listen and repeat.*

1. chicken
2. beef
3. rice
4. vegetables
5. fruit
6. beverages
7. dessert
8. He wants a new job.
9. She wants to see her family.
10. She wants to take a vacation.
11. He wants to start his own business.

2. Pronunciation

chicken

vegetables

beverages

dessert

A Class Party

1 🎧 **Say It** Listen to the conversation. Say it with a partner.

vegetables

A: We're going to have a potluck party. What do you want to bring?

B: I'm going to bring some <u>vegetables</u>.

A: What kind of vegetables?

B: Maybe <u>carrots and corn</u>.

A: That's a good idea.

Practice more conversations. Use the pictures below.

1. fruit

2. beverages

3. dessert

Note: A potluck party = a party where all the guests bring food to share.

2 **Teamwork Task** Work in teams of three or four. Complete the chart with foods you know. Don't use a dictionary.

VEGETABLES	BEVERAGES	FRUIT	DESSERT

3 Say It Listen to the conversation. Say it with a partner.

chicken and rice

A: What is <u>Marco</u> going to bring to the party?

B: <u>He's</u> going to bring <u>chicken and rice</u>.

A: <u>Chicken and rice</u>?

B: Yes. That's a popular food in <u>his</u> country.

Practice more conversations. Use the pictures below.

1. egg rolls

2. shrimp fried rice

3. pizza

GRAMMAR CHECK

Future with *going to*

Use *be* + *going to* + a verb to talk about the future.

Subject	be	going to	Base verb	
I	am	going to	bring	chicken.
You	are	going to	bring	vegetables.
He/She	is	going to	make	dessert.
We	are	going to	make	a salad.
They	are	going to	buy	beverages.

Check Point:

✓ Question = What **are you going to** bring?

4 Write Write the names of the food in the picture. Use these words: *oranges, apples, beans, milk, butter, ice cream, grapes, cake, mashed potatoes, bananas, lettuce, bread, tomatoes, cheese, and strawberries.*

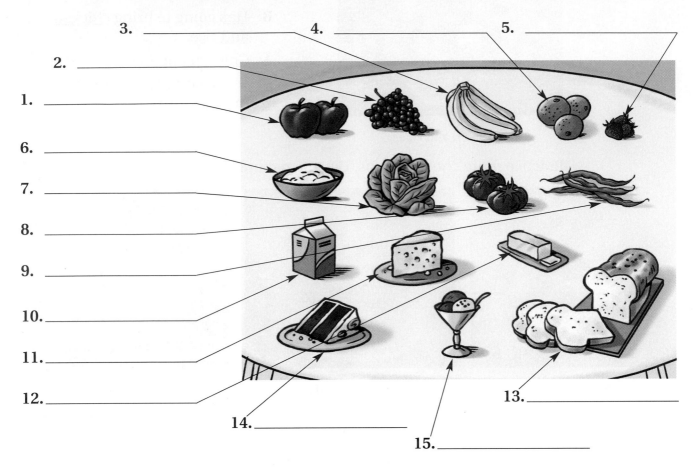

3. _____

4. _____

5. _____

2. _____

1. _____

6. _____

7. _____

8. _____

9. _____

10. _____

11. _____

12. _____

13. _____

14. _____

15. _____

5 Listen Listen and check your answers.

6 Pair Practice Work with a partner. Ask and answer questions about the food in the picture.

Example: *Student 1:* Do you like apples?
Student 2: Yes, I do. *OR* No, I don't.

7 Write Answer the questions about food in your country.

1. What foods do you eat a lot? _____

2. What fruits do you eat a lot? _____

3. What vegetables do you eat a lot? _____

4. What is a popular beverage? _____

8 **Say It** Listen to the conversation. Say it with a partner.

fruit

A: What's your favorite <u>fruit</u>?

B: I don't know, maybe <u>grapes or bananas</u>. How about you?

A: My favorite <u>fruit</u> is _____ .

Practice more conversations. Use the pictures below.

1. beverage   2. dessert   3. vegetable

9 **Teamwork Task** Work in teams of four. Pretend you are having a potluck party with your class. What are you going to bring to the party? Complete the chart.

NAME	FOOD

Tell your teacher what your teammates are going to bring.

Game Time

Your teacher will write the name of a food he or she is going to eat tomorrow. Ask yes/no questions to find out what it is.

Example: *Student 1:* Are you going to eat a vegetable tomorrow?
Teacher: Yes, I am.
Student 1: Are you going to eat potatoes?
Teacher: No, I'm not.
Student 2: Are you going to eat corn?
Teacher: Yes, I am. You win!

Future Plans

1 **Say It** Listen to the conversation. Say it with a partner.

A: What are your plans for the future?

B: I want to get a better job. What are your plans?

A: I want to take a vacation.

B: That's a good idea.

get a better job / take a vacation

Practice more conversations. Use the pictures below.

1. **study English for another year /
visit my family**

2. **go to college /
start my own business**

2 **Pronunciation** Listen and repeat.

The pronunciation of *want to* is often reduced to /wanna/.
   I /*wanna*/ get a better job.
The pronunciation of *going to* is often reduced to /gonna/.
   She's /*gonna*/ take a vacation.

1. I *want to* visit my family.
2. I *want to* study English.
3. I'm *going to* bring some vegetables.
4. She's *going to* bring dessert.

Word Help: Vocational classes
Vocational classes are classes that train you for a special job.

---

3 Write Answer the questions about you. Write complete sentences.

DO YOU WANT TO . . .

1. take another English class? <u>Yes, I want to take another English class.</u>

2. go to a university? _____

3. take some vocational classes? _____

4. get a new job? _____

5. take a vacation? _____

4 Read Read about *dos* and *don'ts* at a job interview.

DO	DON'T
Arrive on time.	Arrive late for the interview.
Introduce yourself.	Chew gum.
Wear professional clothes.	Wear shorts or jeans.
Shake hands with the interviewer.	Smoke.
Smile and be polite.	Wear a hat or sunglasses.
Make eye contact with the interviewer.	Talk about personal things.
Speak slowly and clearly.	Mumble or talk too quietly.

GRAMMAR CHECK

Future questions and short answers

Questions	Answers
Are you going to arrive on time?	Yes, I am.
Is she going to smile?	Yes, she is.
Are we going to sit up straight?	Yes, we are.
Are they going to speak slowly?	Yes, they are.

5 Write Write what Monica is going to do at her job interview.

1. Is she going to shake hands with the interviewer? <u>Yes,</u>

2. Is she going to wear sunglasses? _____

3. Is she going to be polite? _____

4. Is she going to talk about her husband? _____

5. Is she going to arrive on time? _____

6. Is she going to chew gum? _____

Write three more things Monica is going to do and three more things that she isn't going to do.

6 **Pair Practice** Work with a partner. Ask and answer questions about Monica's job interview.

Example: *Student 1:* Is Monica going to introduce herself?
Student 2: Yes, she is.

7 **Say It** Listen to the conversation. Say it with a partner.

arrive on time

A: I'm going to a job interview so I have to get ready.

B: What do you have to do?

A: I have to fill out an application.

B: What else?

A: I have to <u>arrive on time</u>. That's very important.

Practice more conversations. Use the pictures below.

1. **wear clean business clothes**

2. **shake hands with the interviewer**

GRAMMAR CHECK

have to		
Use *have to* to show necessity.		
Subject	**have to**	**Base verb**
I/You/We/They	have to	fill out	an application.
He/She	has to	wear	nice clothes.

8 **Listen** Listen and circle *good idea* or *bad idea*.

1. good idea   bad idea
2. good idea   bad idea
3. good idea   bad idea
4. good idea   bad idea
5. good idea   bad idea
6. good idea   bad idea

1. Marco   2. Monica   3. Jenny   4. Han

9 Write Answer the questions with complete sentences.

1. What is Marco's first goal?   <u>He wants to</u> _____ .
2. What is Jenny's first goal? _____
3. What is Jenny's second goal? _____
4. Who wants to go to a vocational school? _____
5. Who wants to become a teacher? _____
6. Who wants to travel to another country? _____
7. Does Han want to work in an office? _____
8. Does Marco want to have his own business? _____

10 Teamwork Task Work in teams of four or five. Tell about two or three of your future plans. Use *want to*. Then complete the chart.

Example: I want to take more English classes.

NAME	FUTURE PLANS

Tell your teacher about your teammates' plans.

A New Job

1 Say It Listen to the conversation. Say it with a partner.

A: Good morning. Are you a new employee?

B: Yes, I am.

A: Please <u>sign in</u>. You have to <u>sign in</u> every day when you arrive.

B: OK. Thanks.

Practice more conversations. Use the pictures below.

1.

2.

3.

GRAMMAR CHECK

not have to

Use *not have to* when something is not necessary.

Subject	do	not have to	Base verb	
I/We/You/They	do	not have to	wear	a hard hat.
He/She	does	not have to	wear	a hard hat.

Check Point:

✓ Use contractions: I **don't have to** wear a hard hat.

   She **doesn't have to** wear a hard hat.

2 Write Write what is necessary in your class. Use *have to* and *don't have to*.

DO YOU HAVE TO . . .

1. sign in? _____

2. turn off your cell phone? _____

3. bring a notebook? _____

4. buy a textbook? _____

5. sit in the same chair every day? _____

3 **Read** Read the work schedule.

MONICA'S WORK SCHEDULE	
8:15 AM	arrive and sign in
8:30 AM–9:30 AM	visit classrooms
9:30 AM–10:30 AM	help teachers with attendance
10:30 AM–10:45 AM	break
10:45 AM–11:30 AM	correct tests
11:30 AM–1:00 PM	help students with reading
1:00 PM–1:45 PM	lunch
1:45 PM–3:00 PM	help students with writing

4 **Write** Answer the questions about Monica's work schedule.

1. What time does Monica have to arrive? _____

2. What time does Monica visit classrooms? _____

3. What does Monica do at 9:30? _____

4. What does Monica do after her break? _____

5. What does Monica do from 11:30 to 1:00? _____

6. What does Monica have to do after lunch? _____

7. What time does Monica finish work? _____

5 **Listen** Listen and complete the class schedule for Ping.

PING'S CLASS SCHEDULE	
8:00 AM	_____ and hand in _____ .
8:15 AM	_____ vocabulary words.
8:30 AM	
8:45 AM	
9:00 AM	_____ _____ about the story.
9:30 AM	

6 **Pair Practice** Work with a partner. Ask and answer questions about Ping's class schedule.

Example: *Student 1:* What time does Ping have to arrive for class?
Student 2: She has to arrive at 8:00.

Write Read the pay stub and answer the questions.

PAYMENT RECEIPT		ᴧᴧᴧᴧᴧ **DOWN**TOWN**Café**	
EMPLOYEE:		REGULAR HOURS:.....	80
Marco Lopez		RATE:.....................	$12.50/hour
ID:		GROSS PAY:...........	$1,000.00
569988		Federal	
DATE:		withholding:........	$130.00
February 1-14		**NET PAY:**...........	**$870.00**

1. Whose pay stub is this? _____

2. Who is Marco's employer? _____

3. How many hours did Marco work? _____

4. How many hours does he work per week? _____

5. How much does he make per hour? _____

6. How much is his gross pay? _____

7. How much is his check for (net pay)? _____

8 **Write** Read the W2 form and answer the questions.

22222	OMB No. 555-0008	
Employer's name, address and zip code Downtown Café 10 Main Street Downtown CA 90292		
	Income	$21,250.00
Employee's first name and last name Marco Lopez		
Employee's address and zip code Marco Lopez 22 Washington Ave. Downtown CA 90201	Federal Tax Withheld	$2,040.00

Form **W-2** **Wage and Tax Statement**   Department of the Treasury—Internal Revenue Service
Copy 1—For Federal Tax Department   **2010**

1. Whose W2 form is this? _____

2. How much money did he make in 2010? _____

3. How much federal tax did he pay? _____

Note: Employers have to send their employees a W2 form in January.
Employees have to send a copy of the W2 form when they complete
their tax return every year.

> **Word Help: At a job interview**
> **friendly:** likes to meet and talk to new people
> **punctual:** arrives on time
> **independent:** can work alone
> **reliable:** does what he or she is supposed to do
> **patient:** calm, doesn't get upset easily
> **a fast learner:** learns new things quickly

9 **Write** Write sentences. Use *is* or *isn't* and a word from the box.

1. Marco always arrives on time for work. <u>Marco is</u> _____

2. Han always finishes his work before he goes home. _____

3. Julia doesn't like to work alone. _____

4. Monica learns quickly. _____

5. Tanya loves to meet new people. _____

6. Carlos gets upset very easily. _____

10 **Pair Practice** Work with a partner. Ask and answer questions. Use the words from the box.

Example: *Student 1:* Are you friendly?
Student 2: Yes, I am. I like to meet and talk to new people.

11 **Group Practice** Work with a large group or the whole class.

A. Write a word from the Word Help box that describes you.

B. Talk to your classmates. Find one student for each word.

Example: *Student 1:* Are you friendly?
Student 2: Yes, I am. (Write Student 2's name next to *friendly*.)

	NAME
friendly	
punctual	
reliable	
patient	
independent	
a fast learner	

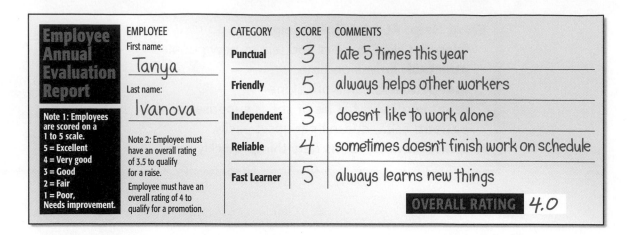

Employee Annual Evaluation Report	EMPLOYEE First name: Tanya Last name: Ivanova	CATEGORY	SCORE	COMMENTS
		Punctual	3	late 5 times this year
		Friendly	5	always helps other workers
		Independent	3	doesn't like to work alone
		Reliable	4	sometimes doesn't finish work on schedule
		Fast Learner	5	always learns new things

Note 1: Employees are scored on a 1 to 5 scale.
5 = Excellent
4 = Very good
3 = Good
2 = Fair
1 = Poor, Needs improvement.

Note 2: Employee must have an overall rating of 3.5 to qualify for a raise.
Employee must have an overall rating of 4 to qualify for a promotion.

OVERALL RATING **4.0**

Word Help: On the job
a raise: more pay
a promotion: a higher (better) job with more responsibilities

---

12 Write Answer the questions about Tanya's employee evaluation.

1. How many times was Tanya late this year? _____

2. Is Tanya sociable? Why? _____

3. Is Tanya independent? Why not? _____

4. What is Tanya's overall score? _____

5. Can Tanya get a raise this year? _____

6. Can Tanya get a promotion this year? _____

---

13 Teamwork Task Work in teams of four or five. Choose a volunteer from your team. Ask the volunteer questions. Complete the evaluation form for the volunteer.

Example: How many times were you late for this class?

Employee Annual Evaluation Report	EMPLOYEE First name: Last name:	CATEGORY	SCORE	COMMENTS
		Punctual		
		Friendly		
		Independent		
		Reliable		
		Fast Learner		

Note 1: Employees are scored on a 1 to 5 scale.
5 = Excellent
4 = Very good
3 = Good
2 = Fair
1 = Poor, Needs improvement.

Note 2: Employee must have an overall rating of 3.5 to qualify for a raise.
Employee must have an overall rating of 4 to qualify for a promotion.

OVERALL RATING

Review

1 **Read and Listen** Read the story. Listen to the story.

Future Plans

Monica is going to a job interview next week. She wants to be a teacher assistant. She is going to wear a nice business suit. She is going to arrive fifteen minutes early. She is going to shake hands with the interviewer and tell about her skills and her work experience. She is going to be polite and friendly. She really wants a job as a teacher assistant.

Alison is going to have a party in her class next week. She is going to buy some paper plates and plastic cups. She is going to make a big salad and buy a pizza. She is going to ask her students to bring some popular food that people eat in their countries. Alison wants her students to have a nice good-bye party.

Ping has some interesting plans for the future. First, she is going to go to college for one semester. Then she is going to take a break from school. She is going to study at home because she is going to have a baby. She is going to stay home for a while and take care of her baby. She wants to be a good mother.

2 **Write** Circle *true* or *false*. Rewrite the false sentences to make them true.

1. Monica is a teacher assistant.	True	False
2. Monica is wearing a business suit now.	True	False
3. Monica is going to tell the interviewer about her work skills.	True	False
4. Alison is going to have a party at her house next week.	True	False
5. Alison is going to make a pizza.	True	False
6. Ping has some plans for the future.	True	False
7. Ping is going to be a mother.	True	False
8. Ping wants to be a good mother.	True	False

3 Write Write sentences. Name the food and the kind of food.

1. Marco is going to bring carrots and corn.

   <u>He's going to bring vegetables.</u>

   _____

   _____

2. What is Monica going to bring to the party?

   _____

   _____

   _____

3. What is Tanya going to bring to the party?

   _____

   _____

   _____

4. What is Carlos going to bring to the party?

   _____

   _____

   _____

4 Write What is Tanya going to do at her job interview? Write two sentences under each picture.

1. _____   2. _____

   _____   _____

5 Best Answer Bubble the correct answers.

	a	b	c
	○	○	○

1. What kind of vegetables is he going to bring?
   a) Apples and corn.
   b) Carrots and oranges.
   c) Carrots and corn.

2. What are your plans for the summer?
   I'm _____ to take a vacation.
   a) going   b) want   c) need

3. Is he going to arrive on time? Yes, he _____ .
   a) has   b) have to   c) is

4. She's going to apply for a job. She _____ fill out
   an application.
   a) has to   b) going to   c) have to

5. Are you a new employee? Yes, I _____ .
   a) can   b) do   c) am

6. She likes to meet new people. She's _____ .
   a) independent   b) friendly   c) patient

6 Write Correct the mistakes in the sentences. If there are no mistakes,
write *correct*.

1. My favorite vegetable is ice cream.

   _____

2. We going to have a party. Do you want to come?

   _____

3. I don't want take another English class.

   _____

4. Please arrive on time for the interview.

   _____

5. It's a good idea to wear a hat to a job interview.

   _____

6. All employees have sign in when they arrive.

   _____

7. She's very friendly. She always arrives on time.

   _____

7 Teamwork Task Work in teams of four or five. Ask your teammates about their future plans. Complete the chart.

NAME	FUTURE PLANS

8 Teamwork Task Work in teams of four. Complete the evaluation form for your team. Ask your teammates questions. Then write a number from 1 to 5 for each category (1 = the worst; 5 = the best).

Example: *Student 1:* How many times were you late to class?
Student 2: I was never late. (Write *5* for punctual.)

EVALUATION FORM				
Name				
punctual				
friendly				
independent				
reliable				
Overall Rating				

I can . . .			
• identify foods and food groups.	1	2	3
• talk about future plans.	1	2	3
• talk about likes and dislikes.	1	2	3
• identify *dos* and *don'ts* for a job interview.	1	2	3
• understand workplace expectations in the U.S.	1	2	3
• read a work schedule.	1	2	3
• understand a pay stub.	1	2	3
• interpret a W2 form.	1	2	3
• use personality adjectives at a job interview.	1	2	3
• understand an employee evaluation form.	1	2	3
• complete an employee evaluation form.	1	2	3

1 = not well   2 = OK   3 = very well

DOWNTOWN

Ping: How was your job (1) _____ , Monica?
Monica: Great. I got the job. I'm (2) _____ to be a teacher assistant next semester.

Ping: How about you, Jenny? What (3) _____ you going to do next?
Jenny: I'm going back to Colombia. I (4) _____ to see my family. I miss my family a lot.

Ping: What are your (5) _____ for the future, Ms. Ryan?
Alison: Next week (6) _____ going to take a nice long vacation. That's my only plan.

Ping: I'd like to take a vacation too, but I (7) _____ . I (8) _____ prepare a room for my baby. I want to be a really good mother.

Tanya: I have some new plans, too. Michael and I are going to get married.
Ping: You are? When?
Tanya: In October. (9) _____ going to have a big wedding, and you are all invited.

Alison: I want to say that all of your plans are wonderful, and I (10) _____ going to miss all of you very much!

 Group Practice Work in a group of five. Practice the story.

Audio Script

CHAPTER 1: **Names and Numbers**

Page 3 (Chapter Opening)

Listen *Listen and repeat.*

A B C D E F G H I J K L M N O P Q R
S T U V W X Y Z

Page 4 (Lesson 1, Activity 1)

Say It *Listen to the conversation. Say it with your teacher. Use your name.*

A: Hello. I am your teacher. My name is
Alison Ryan.
B: Hello. My name is Ping Chang.
A: Nice to meet you, Ping.
B: Nice to meet you, too.

Page 5 (Lesson 1, Activity 5)

Pronunciation *Listen and repeat.*

A   E   I   O   U   Y

Page 5 (Lesson 1, Activity 6)

Listen *Listen. Circle the letter you hear.*

1. A   6. i
2. E   7. a
3. Y   8. w
4. I   9. a
5. U   10. e

Page 5 (Lesson 1, Activity 7)

Listen *Listen. Write the missing letters.*

1. My first name is Tanya. T-A-N-Y-A.
2. My last name is Lopez. L-O-P-E-Z.
3. A: My full name is Monica Silva.
   B: How do you spell that?
   A: Monica. M-O-N-I-C-A. My last name is
   Silva. S-I-L-V-A.

Page 6 (Lesson 1, Activity 8)

Say It *Listen to the conversation. Say it with a partner.*

A: Hello. My name is Han Do.
B: I'm sorry. What's your first name?
A: Han. H-A-N.
B: Nice to meet you, Han. I am Tanya.
A: Nice to meet you, too, Tanya.

Page 8 (Lesson 2, Activity 1)

Listen *Listen and repeat the numbers.*

0 1 2 3 4 5 6 7 8 9 10
11 12 13 14 15 16 17 18 19
20 30 40 50 60 70 80 90 100

Page 8 (Lesson 2, Activity 2)

Pronunciation *Listen and repeat the numbers.*

1. 13 / 30
2. 14 / 40
3. 15 / 50
4. 16 / 60
5. 17 / 70
6. 18 / 80
7. 19 / 90

Page 9 (Lesson 2, Activity 3)

Say It *Listen to the conversation. Say it with a partner.*

A: What is your telephone number?
B: My telephone number?
A: Yes.
B: My area code is eight, one, eight.
A: And the phone number?
B: My phone number is five, five, five—three,
two, three, zero.

Page 9 (Lesson 2, Activity 4)

Listen *Listen and circle the number you hear.*

1. 30   5. 17
2. 18   6. 60
3. 40   7. 90
4. 16   8. 15

Page 10 (Lesson 2, Activity 6)

Say It *Listen to the conversations. Say them with a partner.*

A: What is his telephone number?
B: His area code is eight, one, eight.
A: And his phone number?
B: His phone number is five, five, five—nine,
eight, five, zero.

A: What is her telephone number?
B: Her area code is three, one, zero.
A: And her phone number?
B: Her phone number is five, five, five—eight,
five, one, three.

Page 11 (Lesson 2, Activity 7)

Say It *Listen to the conversation. Say it with a partner.*

A: What's your address?
B: My address is 324 Rose Avenue.
A: How do you spell that?
B: Rose, R-O-S-E, Avenue.
A: Thank you.
B: You're welcome.

Page 11 (Lesson 2, Activity 8)

Listen *Listen and write the missing numbers.*

1. My address is three thirteen Avenue A.
2. My phone number is two, one, three—five, five, five—sixty-five, fifty.
3. His area code is three, one, zero. His phone number is five, five, five—three, nine, six, two.
4. Her address is twenty-three fifteen Rose Avenue. Her apartment number is eight.
5. Their phone number is four, one, five—five, five, five—twelve, sixty.

Page 13 (Lesson 3, Activity 1)

Say It *Listen to the conversation. Say it with a partner.*

A: Who is she?
B: She is my classmate. Her name is Ping.
A: Where is she from?
B: She is from China.

Page 14 (Lesson 3, Activity 2)

Say It *Listen to the conversation. Say it with a partner.*

A: Who are they?
B: They are my classmates.
A: Where are they from?
B: They are from Mexico. Their native language is Spanish.

Page 15 (Lesson 3, Activity 4)

Pronunciation *Listen and repeat the contractions.*

I'm	I'm a teacher.
You're	You're a student.
He's	He's my classmate.
She's	She's from Mexico.
It's	It's my telephone number.
We're	We're from Brazil.
They're	They're students.

Page 17 (Chapter Review, Activity 1)

Read and Listen *Read the story. Listen to the story.*

My Classmates

Hello. I am Ping. My last name is Chang. I am from China. My English teacher is Alison Ryan. She is from New York. English is her native language. Carlos Garcia is one of my classmates. He is from El Salvador. Spanish is his native language. Marco and Carolina are from Mexico. Spanish is their native language, too. Han is from Vietnam, and Tanya is from Russia.

My classmates are from ten different countries. How many different countries are your classmates from?

Page 18 (Chapter Review, Activity 3)

Listen *Listen to the conversation. Write the missing information on the student registration form.*

A: What's your name?
B: My last name is Vidal. My first name is Jenny. J-E-N-N-Y. My middle initial is A.
A: And your address?
B: My address is six eleven Tree Street.
A: Is it an apartment?
B: Yes. My apartment number is 9.
A: What city and state?
B: My city is Santa Monica. My state is California. And my zip code is nine, zero, four, zero, five.
A: What's your telephone number?
B: The area code is three, one, oh. And the number is five, five, five—twenty-two, eighteen.
A: What's your native country?
B: My native country?
A: Yes. Where are you from?
B: Colombia. My native language is Spanish.

CHAPTER 2: **School**

Page 23 (Chapter Opening, Activity 1)

Listen *Listen and repeat.*

1. a teacher	10. a table
2. a student	11. a chair
3. a chalkboard	12. a notebook
4. a piece of chalk	13. a dictionary
5. an eraser	14. a computer
6. a desk	15. a clock
7. a book	16. a trash can
8. a pencil	17. a bookcase
9. a pen	

Page 23 (Chapter Opening, Activity 2)

Listen *Listen and point to the words in the picture.*

1. a teacher	10. a table
2. a student	11. a chair
3. a chalkboard	12. a notebook
4. a piece of chalk	13. a dictionary
5. an eraser	14. a computer
6. a desk	15. a clock
7. a book	16. a trash can
8. a pencil	17. a bookcase
9. a pen	

Page 23 (Chapter Opening, Activity 3)

Pronunciation

teacher	table
student	notebook
chalkboard	dictionary
eraser	computer
pencil	bookcase

Say It *Listen to the conversations. Say them with a partner.*

A: What's this?
B: It's a pen.

A: What's that?
B: It's a chair.

Say It *Listen to the conversation. Say it with a partner.*

A: What are they?
B: They are books.
A: How many books?
B: Three books.

Say It *Listen to the conversations. Say them with a partner.*

A: Is that a pencil?
B: Yes, it is.

A: Is that a pencil?
B: No, it's not. It's a pen.

Say It *Listen to the conversations. Say them with a partner.*

A: Are they pencils?
B: Yes, they are.

A: Are they pencils?
B: No, they're not. They are pens.

Listen *Listen. Circle the word you hear.*

1. A: What's that?
   B: It's a pen.
2. A: What's that?
   B: That's my notebook.
3. A: What's this?
   B: It's a desk.
4. A: What's that called?
   B: That's a chalkboard.
5. A: What's that over there?
   B: It's a clock.
6. A: Who is she?
   B: She's a teacher.

Say It *Listen to the conversation. Say it with a partner.*

A: Who is she?
B: That's Ms. Ryan.
A: Is she a student?
B: No, she isn't. She's a teacher.
A: Oh. My mistake!

Pronunciation *Listen and repeat the titles.*

1. Mr.   Mr. Jones   3. Miss   Miss Jones
2. Ms.   Ms. Jones   4. Mrs.   Mrs. Jones

Say It *Listen to the conversation. Say it with a partner.*

A: Is Ms. Ryan in the classroom?
B: No, she isn't.
A: Where is she?
B: She's in the office.

Say It *Listen to the conversation. Say it with a partner.*

A: Is the dictionary on the desk?
B: No, it isn't.
A: Where is it?
B: It's in the trash can.
A: Please put it on the desk.
B: OK.

Listen *Listen and write the names of the students in the correct places.*

A: Tell me about your class. Who are the students in your class?
B: Well, I'll tell you about the students who are my friends. The first is Monica. She sits in the front of the class near the teacher. Ping sits next to Monica. Carolina sits next to Ping. Marco is behind Carolina, and Carlos is in back of Marco. Tanya and Han are behind Monica. Tanya is in front of Han. Julia is between Han and Carlos. And the last one is Jenny. Jenny is between Julia and Ping. And, of course, Ms. Ryan is the teacher. She is in front of all the students.
A: It sounds like a nice class.
B: It is.

Say It *Listen to the conversation. Say it with two partners.*

A: This is Mr. Bell. He is a counselor.
B: Hello, Mr. Bell. How are you today?
C: I'm fine, thank you. How are you?
B: I'm very good.

Say It *Listen to the conversation. Say it with a partner.*

A: Please write your name.
B: Write my name?
A: Yes. Write your name in your notebook.
B: OK.

Listen *Listen. Follow the directions. Write in the box.*

1. Write your first name next to number one.
2. Write these letters next to number 2: A, E, I, O and U.
3. Write number 9 under letter A.
4. Write number 5 under letter I.
5. Write number 3 between number 9 and number 5.

6. Circle the letter E.
7. Underline the letter U.
8. Write your address under your name.
9. Sign your name next to the letter X.
10. Write your zip code between your address and your signature.
11. Write your classroom number next to your zip code.
12. Write your teacher's name under your classroom number.
13. Raise your hand if you have no mistakes.

Page 37 (Chapter Review, Activity 1)

Read and Listen *Read the story. Listen to the story.*

My Classroom

Hello again. This is Ping. I am in my English class right now. Ten other students are in my classroom, too. My friend, Monica, is next to me. Tanya is behind her, and Marco is behind Tanya. Ms. Ryan, my teacher, is in front of the class. The door is open. Mr. Bell, the counselor, is next to the door. "Good morning, Ms. Ryan," he says. "How are you?"

"I'm fine," she says. "How are you?"

The chalkboard is behind Ms. Ryan. Her name is on the chalkboard. The name of our class, ESL 1, is under her name. There is a piece of chalk in Ms. Ryan's hand. Two pens and ten pencils are on her desk. An English book is on her desk, too. "Please open your books," Ms. Ryan says. The name of my book is *Downtown*. I think it's a great book!

Page 39 (Chapter Review, Activity 7)

Listen *Listen and write in the box below.*

Write your first name next to number 1.
Write the letter Z next to number 2.
Write your teacher's title between your first name and the letter Z.
Write your last name under Z.
Write the name of your English book next to number 3.
Write your native country between your first name and the name of your English book.
Write your title under your teacher's title.
Write your address under your last name.
Write the number of students that are in class today between your address and the name of your textbook.

Page 39 (Chapter Review, Activity 8)

Pronunciation *Listen and repeat the words. Stress the correct syllables.*

teacher	notebook	dictionary
computer	classroom	between

Now listen and underline the stressed syllable in these words:

eraser	pencil	table
bookcase	behind	student

Say the words again.

CHAPTER 3: **Time**

Page 43 (Chapter Opening, Activity 1)

Listen *Listen and repeat.*

1. a month
2. a year
3. a day
4. a date
5. a holiday
6. a time
7. an appointment

Page 43 (Chapter Opening, Activity 2)

Listen *Listen to the words. Look at the picture. Repeat.*

1. a month—January
2. a year—2009
3. a day—Monday
4. a date—January 3rd
5. a holiday—New Year's Day
6. a time—8:00
7. an appointment—Dr. Gray at 2:30 on January 8th

Page 43 (Chapter Opening, Activity 3)

Pronunciation

holiday	appointment

Page 44 (Lesson 1, Activity 1)

Say It *Listen to the conversation. Say it with a partner.*

A: What time is it?
B: It's three o'clock.
A: What time is your appointment?
B: Three-fifteen.
A: That's good. You're on time.

Page 45 (Lesson 1, Activity 2)

Say It *Listen to the conversation. Say it with a partner.*

A: What time is it?
B: It's a quarter after one.
A: I'm sorry. What time is it?
B: It's one-fifteen.
A: What time is your appointment?
B: One o'clock.
A: That's bad. You're late!

Page 46 (Lesson 1, Activity 3)

Listen *Listen and write the times. Then draw the hands on the clocks.*

1. A: What time is it?
   B: It's six-forty-five.
   A: Six-forty-five?
   B: Yes, that's right.
2. A: What time is it?
   B: It's three-twenty.
   A: Three-twenty?
   B: Exactly.
3. A: What time is it?
   B: It's a quarter to five.
   A: A quarter to *five*?
   B: Yes, that's right.

4. A: What time is it?
   B: It's five-fifty-five.
   A: I'm sorry. What time?
   B: Five minutes to six.
5. A: What time is it?
   B: It's a quarter after nine.
   A: A quarter *after* nine?
   B: Yes, that's right.
6. A: What time is it?
   B: It's five-thirty.
   A: Five-thirteen?
   B: No. Five-thirty.

Page 48 (Lesson 2, Activity 1)

Listen *Listen and repeat the days of the week.*

Sunday, Monday, Tuesday, Wednesday, Thursday, Friday, Saturday.

Page 48 (Lesson 2, Activity 2)

Say It *Listen to the conversation. Say it with a partner.*

A: What day is today?
B: It's Monday.
A: Monday? Are you sure?
B: Yes, I am. Today is Monday and tomorrow is Tuesday.

Page 49 (Lesson 2, Activity 4)

Say It *Listen to the conversation. Say it with a partner.*

A: When is your class?
B: On Monday and Wednesday.
A: What time?
B: Eight o'clock.
A: How long is it?
B: It's three hours—from eight o'clock to eleven o'clock.

Page 50 (Lesson 2, Activity 6)

Listen *Listen and write the days and times.*

1. A: When is Ms. Ryan's ESL 2 English class?
   B: It's on Saturday.
   A: What time on Saturday?
   B: From 9 a.m. to1 p.m..
2. A: When is Ms. Jeronymo's pronunciation class?
   B: It's from Monday to Friday.
   A: What time does it start?
   B: 11:30 in the morning.
3. A: When is the new computer class?
   B: It's four days a week—from Monday to Thursday.
   A: What time?
   B: From 10 a.m. to 3 p.m..
4. A: I'm looking for the new writing class with Anita West. I think it's a weekend class.
   B: Yes. That class meets on Saturday and Sunday only.
   A: What time?
   B: The class goes from 2:30 to 4:45 in the afternoon.

A: That's a good time. Thank you very much.
B: My pleasure.

Page 52 (Lesson 3, Activity 1)

Listen *Listen and repeat the months of the year.*

January	February	March
April	May	June
July	August	September
October	November	December

Page 52 (Lesson 3, Activity 2)

Say It *Listen to the conversation. Say it with a partner.*

A: When is Ping's birthday?
B: It's in April.
A: What's the date?
B: It's on April first.

Page 53 (Lesson 3, Activity 4)

Listen *Listen and repeat the ordinal numbers.*

first, second, third, fourth, fifth, sixth, seventh, eighth, ninth, tenth, eleventh, twelfth, thirteenth, fourteenth, fifteenth, sixteenth, seventeenth, eighteenth, nineteenth, twentieth, twenty-first, twenty-second, twenty-third, twenty-fourth, twenty-fifth, twenty-sixth, twenty-seventh, twenty-eighth, twenty-ninth, thirtieth, thirty-first

Page 53 (Lesson 3, Activity 5)

Pronunciation *Listen and repeat the words with a /th/ sound.*

three	third	Thursday	fourth
fifth	sixth	thirteen	thirty

Page 53 (Lesson 3, Activity 6)

Listen *Listen and write the dates you hear.*

1. August 2nd
2. September 13th
3. March 5th
4. November 21st
5. July 30th
6. October 3rd
7. June 14th
8. February 9th
9. January 28th
10. April 29th

Page 54 (Lesson 3, Activity 8)

Say It *Listen to the conversation. Say it with a partner.*

A: What is Ping's date of birth?
B: Her birthday is on April first.
A: What year was she born?
B: She was born in 1982. So, her date of birth is April first, nineteen eighty-two.

Page 55 (Lesson 3, Activity 10)

Say It *Listen to the conversation. Say it with a partner.*

A: Independence Day is a holiday in the United States.
B: When is Independence Day?
A: It's in July.
B: What day in July?
A: It's on July fourth.

Listen *Listen and write the dates of the holidays.*

1. A: When is Labor Day?
   B: It's on the first Monday in September.
2. A: When is Thanksgiving?
   B: Thanksgiving is on the fourth Thursday in November.
3. A: When is Presidents' Day?
   B: It's on the third Monday in February.
4. A: When is Memorial Day?
   B: It's on the last Monday in May.
5. A: When is Christmas Day?
   B: It's on December 25th.

Read and Listen *Read and listen to the story. Underline the dates.*

Birthdays

All of Ping's friends in her English class have birthdays in different months. Julia's birthday is on January first, New Year's Day. Tanya's birthday is in February, on the fourteenth. That's Valentine's Day. Han Do's birthday is on March fifteenth. And, of course, Ping's birthday is in April, on the first. Her date of birth is 4/1/82.

Carlos has a birthday in the spring, on May 5th. That's a holiday in Mexico. Jenny's birthday is on the first day of summer, June 21. And Marco's birthday is on 7/3, the day before Independence Day. The fourth of July is a big holiday in the United States. It's the birthday of the country. The U.S. is more than 200 years old. Monica's birthday is in September, on the second. She isn't 200 years old. She's only 29.

Today is October 6th. It is a Thursday and it is a special day for Ms. Ryan because today is her birthday. Right now it is 11:00 and that's a good time for a birthday party for Ms. Ryan's special day. So...

"Happy birthday to you,
Happy birthday to you,
Happy birthday, Ms. Ryan,
Happy birthday to you!"

Listen *Listen and write the days, dates, and times.*

1. A: Hello. I'm interested in an English class.
   B: English classes are available on Monday, Wednesday, and Friday.
   A: What time?
   B: We have morning classes from 8:20 to 12:00 noon.
   A: Do you have evening classes?
   B: Yes, we have evening classes, too. The evening classes start at 6:05 in the evening. They end at 9:15.
   A: When does the class start?
   B: Classes begin on Monday, September 22nd.
   A: OK. Thank you very much.

2. A: I'd like to take an ESL conversation class. What day is the conversation class?
   B: We have classes from Monday to Thursday.
   A: Do you have morning classes?
   B: Yes. It is a morning class. It starts at 10:15 and ends at 11:45.
   A: Great. When can I start?
   B: The class begins on October 3rd.

CHAPTER 4: **Shopping**

Listen *Listen and repeat.*

1. a jacket
2. a blouse
3. pants
4. shoes
5. a suit
6. a sweater
7. jeans
8. boots
9. a dress
10. a belt
11. shorts
12. a T-shirt
13. sneakers

Pronunciation

jacket   sweater   sneakers

Say It *Listen to the conversation. Say it with a partner.*

A: How much is this?
B: It's ten dollars.
A: Are you sure?
B: Yes, I'm positive. It's a ten-dollar bill.

Say It *Listen to the conversation. Say it with a partner.*

A: How much are the T-shirts?
B: They're ten dollars and fifty cents.
A: How much do you have?
B: I have twenty dollars.
A: Great.

Listen *Listen and write the money in the boxes.*

1. A: Alison, do you have any money?
   B: Yes, a little. Let me see. I have a twenty-dollar bill, and also a five, and two ones. How much do you need?
   A: More than that.
2. A: Marco, do you have any money?
   B: Yes, Jenny, I do. I have a nickel, and a dime. How about you? Do you have any money?
   A: I have a quarter.
   B: That's not very much, is it?
3. A: Ping, do you have any money I can borrow?
   B: Sure. Let's see. I have a twenty, two tens, a five, and some change. How much do you need?

4. A: How much money do you have, Han?
B: You mean right now? In my pocket?
A: Yes.
B: Well, let's see. I have a five-dollar bill and three singles. And I have two quarters, a dime, and a nickel. How about pennies?
A: You can keep the pennies!

Page 68 (Lesson 2, Activity 1)

Listen *Listen and repeat the colors. Then point at something in your classroom for each color.*

red	orange	yellow	green	blue
purple	pink	brown	white	black

Page 69 (Lesson 2, Activity 5)

Say It *Listen to the conversation. Say it with a partner.*

A: I need a new pair of shorts.
B: What color shorts do you want?
A: I like red.
B: Here's a pair of red shorts.
A: Thanks.

Page 70 (Lesson 2, Activity 7)

Say It *Listen to the conversation. Say it with a partner.*

A: Jenny wants a new leather jacket.
B: What color does she want?
A: She wants black or brown.
B: What size does she need?
A: She needs a small.

Page 73 (Lesson 3, Activity 1)

Say It *Listen to the conversation. Say it with a partner.*

A: May I help you?
B: Yes, please. I'm looking for a black leather jacket.
A: Here's a black leather jacket. What size do you need?
B: I need a medium, I think.
A: This is a medium.
B: How much is it?
A: This one is $149.
B: Oh, that's a lot.

Page 74 (Lesson 3, Activity 2)

Say It *Listen to the conversation. Say it with a partner.*

A: Do you like red shoes?
B: No, I don't.
A: What color shoes do you like?
B: I like black or brown shoes. I definitely don't like red shoes!

Page 75 (Lesson 3, Activity 5)

Listen *Listen and complete the chart.*

A: What are your favorite kinds of clothes, Ping?
B: Well, I like blue jeans a lot. And I like dresses sometimes when I go out. I don't like to wear shorts. I'm not comfortable in shorts.

A: So, what do you wear in the summer?
B: I just wear blue or black jeans and a T-shirt most of the time. Or jeans and a light-colored blouse, like yellow or white, and sneakers. I really like comfortable shoes.
A: How about in the winter? Do you like sweaters?
B: No, I don't. I like jackets. I like all kinds of jackets. I like leather jackets or any warm jacket on a cold day.

Page 77 (Chapter Review, Activity 1)

Read and Listen *Read the story. Listen to the story.*

Winter Clothes

It is November. The weather is getting cold. Ping and Jenny are shopping together for winter clothes. Jenny wants a sweater. She wants a pink sweater. Ping doesn't like sweaters very much. But she needs something warm. She wants a jacket. She wants a warm jacket.

The sweaters are very nice. "What size do you need?" Ping asks. Jenny needs a small. "What color do you want?" Ping asks. Jenny wants pink. "This is a really nice one," Ping says. She picks up the sweater.

Jenny looks at it. "It looks great," she says. "But how much is it?"

"It's $89."

"That's too much," Jenny says. "I only have $50." Jenny wants to pay cash. She doesn't like credit cards. "There's a nice jacket," she says, pointing at a rack of jackets.

Ping picks up one jacket. It is warm and black, and it is beautiful. It is a size medium.

"How much is it?" Jenny asks.

"$149."

"That's a lot."

Ping tries on the jacket. It looks great. "It's not too much," she says. "I really like it!" Fortunately, Ping has a credit card.

Page 78 (Chapter Review, Activity 4)

Listen *Listen and check your answers to Activity 3. Then write the prices in the picture.*

a. A: That's a nice belt. How much is it?
   B: $30.
b. A: How much is that shirt?
   B: $45.
c. A: How much are the blue jeans?
   B: Those blue jeans are on sale for $25.
d. A: That's a nice dress. I love the color. What is the price?
   B: This one is $199.
   A: Oh. That's a lot.
e. A: I like that yellow sweater. Is it expensive?
   B: Not very expensive. It's $65.
f. A: I like those shorts. How much are they?
   B: Only $25.

g. A: How much is that suit?
   B: Three ninety-nine.
   A: Three hundred and ninety-nine dollars?
   B: Yes, that's right.
h. A: I love those boots. How much are they?
   B: Eighty-nine dollars. Do you want
      to try them on?
   A: Yes, please.

Page 79 (Chapter Review, Activity 7)

Pronunciation *Plural nouns have three ending sounds: /s/, /z/, and /iz/. Listen and repeat.*

/s/ pants, socks, boots
/z/ shoes, sweaters, jeans
/iz/ dresses, blouses, necklaces

Listen again and write the sound you hear (/s/, /z/, or /iz/).

shirts, shorts, credit cards, jackets, sizes

CHAPTER 5: **Home and Family**

Page 83 (Chapter Opening, Activity 1)

Listen *Listen and repeat.*

1. father   Jenny's father
2. mother   Jenny's mother
3. parents   Jenny's parents
4. grandfather   Jenny's grandfather
5. grandmother   Jenny's grandmother
6. uncle   Jenny's uncle
7. aunt   Jenny's aunt
8. brother   Jenny's brother
9. sister   Jenny's sister
10. husband   Miguel is Martha's husband.
11. wife   Martha is Miguel's wife.

Page 83 (Chapter Opening, Activity 2)

Pronunciation

father   uncle
mother   brother
parents   sister
grandfather   husband
grandmother

Page 84 (Lesson 1, Activity 1)

Say It *Listen to the conversation. Say it with a partner.*

A: Who is that?
B: That's Andrea.
A: Who is Andrea?
B: She is Jenny's sister.

Page 85 (Lesson 1, Activity 4)

Listen *Listen and write sentences about the family relationships.*

1. A: Who is she?
   B: That's Marco's mother.
   A: Marco's mother?
   B: Yes, that's right.

2. A: Who is he?
   B: He is Tanya's grandfather.
   A: Wow. He looks young for a grandfather.
3. A: Who is that boy?
   B: He's Francisco's son.
   A: How old is he?
   B: I think he's about seven.
4. A: Who is that tall man?
   B: That's Ping's husband.
   A: Really?
   B: Really.
5. A: Who are they?
   B: They are Alison's grandparents.
   A: Alison's grandparents? They don't look
      very old.

Page 88 (Lesson 2, Activity 1)

Pronunciation *Listen and repeat.*

1. kitchen   4. bathroom
2. living room   5. bedroom
3. dining room   6. yard

Page 89 (Lesson 2, Activity 3)

Say It *Listen to the conversation. Say it with a partner.*

A: What time is it?
B: It's seven o'clock.
A: Where is Ping?
B: She's in the bathroom.
A: What's she doing?
B: She's taking a shower.

Page 91 (Lesson 2, Activity 7)

Listen *Listen and circle the word you hear.*

1. bedroom   4. watching
2. reading   5. taking
3. talking   6. bathroom

Page 93 (Lesson 3, Activity 1)

Say It *Listen to the conversation. Say it with a partner.*

A: Where is Carlos?
B: He is at work.
A: What is he doing?
B: He is fixing a car.

Page 94 (Lesson 3, Activity 2)

Say It *Listen to the conversation. Say it with a partner.*

A: Is Ping in the kitchen?
B: Yes, she is.
A: Is she cooking?
B: No, she isn't. She is drinking tea.

Page 95 (Lesson 3, Activity 3)

Say It *Listen to the conversation. Say it with a partner.*

A: Where are my parents?
B: They're in the living room.
A: Are they watching a movie?
B: No, they aren't. They're watching the news.

Page 96 (Lesson 3, Activity 4)

Say It *Listen to the conversation. Say it with a partner.*

A: Tell me about Ping's husband. Is he tall or short?
B: He's tall.
A: How tall is he?
B: He's very tall.

Page 97 (Chapter Review, Activity 1)

Read and Listen *Read the story. Listen to the story.*

Happy Anniversary

Today is Jenny's mother and father's 25th wedding anniversary and they are having a party. All of the people in Jenny's family are attending the party except Jenny. Jenny isn't in Colombia. She is living in California. She is going to school and studying English in Los Angeles.

In Colombia, Jenny's father is in the yard. He is cooking chicken for everyone on the barbecue grill. Jenny's Aunt Luisa is talking to everyone and putting dishes on the table. Jenny's sister, Andrea, is making a chocolate cake for the party. Her daughter, Karla, is helping her. Jenny's grandparents are in the living room. They are sitting on the couch and watching TV.

Right now, Jenny's mom is talking on the telephone. She is talking to her daughter in California. She is talking to Jenny.

"I'm sorry I'm not there with you," Jenny says. "But I'm calling to wish you a happy anniversary."

Jenny's mom is smiling. She is smiling because she is looking at her family around her and she is talking to her other daughter on the telephone. "Thank you for calling," Jenny's mom says. "We all miss you."

"I miss you, too," Jenny says.

Page 98 (Chapter Review, Activity 4)

Listen *Listen and write the sentences.*

1. Jenny's aunt is in the living room.
2. Carlos is in the bedroom.
3. Ping is brushing her teeth.
4. Tanya's brother is taking a message.
5. Alison's father is reading the newspaper.
6. Marco is washing the dishes.

Page 99 (Chapter Review, Activity 7)

Pronunciation *Listen and repeat the sentences. Stress the correct syllables.*

1. He's cooking dinner.
2. She's taking a shower.
3. They're watching television.
4. He's washing the dishes.
5. She's listening to music.

CHAPTER 6: **Housing**

Page 103 (Chapter Opening, Activity 1)

Listen *Listen and repeat.*

1. a sofa / a couch
2. a coffee table
3. an armchair
4. a rug
5. a TV
6. a stove
7. a refrigerator
8. a dishwasher
9. cabinets
10. a bed
11. a night table
12. a lamp
13. a dresser
14. a mirror
15. curtains
16. a sink
17. a shower
18. a toilet

Page 103 (Chapter Opening, Activity 2)

Pronunciation

sofa	dresser
armchair	mirror
carpet	curtains
refrigerator	shower
dishwasher	toilet
cabinets	

Page 104 (Lesson 1, Activity 1)

Say It *Listen to the conversation. Say it with a partner.*

A: What's that?
B: It's a lamp.
A: Where is it?
B: It's in the bedroom.
A: There's a lamp in my bedroom, too.

Page 105 (Lesson 1, Activity 2)

Say It *Listen to the conversation. Say it with a partner.*

A: Is there a sofa in your living room?
B: Yes, there is. There's a very nice sofa in my living room. Is there a sofa in your living room?
A: Yes, there is. *OR* No, there isn't.

Page 106 (Lesson 1, Activity 3)

Say It *Listen to the conversation. Say it with a partner.*

A: Are there any cabinets in your kitchen?
B: Yes, there are. Are there any cabinets in your kitchen?
A: Yes, there are. *OR* No, there aren't.

Page 106 (Lesson 1, Activity 5)

Listen *Listen and write the furniture and appliances in the correct rooms below.*

a sofa   a refrigerator
a shower   a night table
a bed   a TV
a coffee table   an armchair
a lamp   a dresser

Page 108 (Lesson 2, Activity 1)

Say It *Listen to the conversation. Say it with a partner.*

A: Is there a stove in Tanya's apartment?
B: Yes, there is.
A: Is it new or old?
B: It's old. It's very old.
A: What does Tanya want?
B: She wants a new stove.

Page 109 (Lesson 2, Activity 3)

Pronunciation *When we use the article* an, *we usually link, or connect, the -n to the beginning of the next word. Listen and repeat the linked pronunciation.*

an apartment
an old stove
an expensive rug

Page 109 (Lesson 2, Activity 4)

Listen *Listen and write the articles and adjectives.*

1. My living room? It's small. It's a small living room.
2. The kitchen? It's a beautiful kitchen.
3. The bathroom? It's an ugly bathroom.
4. My cabinets are new. They're new cabinets.
5. The yard is very large. That's one of the things I like about the house. It has a large yard.
6. What kind of a rug does she have? I don't know. But I'd say it's expensive. It's an expensive rug.

Page 110 (Lesson 2, Activity 6)

Say It *Listen to the conversation. Say it with a partner.*

A: What's the matter?
B: I want to move. I want a new apartment.
A: Why? What's wrong with your apartment?
B: It's too dark. I want an apartment with more light.

Page 111 (Lesson 2, Activity 8)

Listen *Listen and write the prices.*

A: How much is the dresser?
B: That big old dresser? It's twenty dollars.

A: How much is the sofa?
B: That's a real leather sofa. It's one hundred dollars.
A: Oh. That's a lot.

A: How about the night table? How much is that?
B: Give me fifteen dollars and it's yours.

A: How much is that big lamp?
B: Well, I was asking twenty dollars for it. But I'll give you it to you for fifteen if you take it right now.

A: How about that coffee table? I like that. It's very modern.
B: That's a good piece of furniture. How about seventy-five dollars?

A: How about that TV? How much is that?
B: It's an old TV. I'm asking ten dollars for it.

Page 112 (Lesson 2, Activity 10)

Say It *Listen to the conversation. Say it with a partner.*

A: Hello. This is Tanya in Apartment 301.
B: Hello, Tanya. What can I do for you?
A: There isn't any heat in my apartment.
B: Heat?
A: Yes. There isn't any heat.
B: OK. I'll come right over.
A: Thank you.

Page 113 (Lesson 3, Activity 1)

Say It *Listen to the conversation. Say it with a partner.*

A: I'm interested in the apartment for rent. Can I ask a question about it?
B: Sure.
A: Is there a swimming pool?
B: No, I'm afraid there isn't. Sorry.

Page 115 (Lesson 3, Activity 4)

Say It *Listen to the conversation. Say it with a partner.*

A: Hello. I'm calling about the apartment for rent. Is it still available?
B: Yes, it is.
A: How many bedrooms does it have?
B: It has two bedrooms and one bathroom.
A: Is there a pool?
B: Yes, there is.
A: How much is the rent?
B: It's $1,200 a month. Do you want to see it?
A: Yes, please.

Listen *Listen and write the missing information in the ads.*

1. A: Good morning. I'm calling about the house for rent in Malibu. Can you tell me about it?
   B: Yes. It's a three-bedroom house in Malibu. It's near the beach. It has two bathrooms and a small but modern kitchen. There is a fireplace in the living room.
   A: How much is the rent?
   B: It's $3,500 a month. And a $3,500 security deposit is required.
   A: Oh. That's expensive.

2. A: I'm calling about the apartment for rent downtown. Is it still available?
   B: Yes, it is. It's a two-bedroom apartment—very nice place. It's near a bus stop and the metro line. It has large windows. It's a very bright apartment.
   A: How about the kitchen?
   B: The kitchen is nice. There is a new stove and refrigerator. And it has a remodeled bathroom.
   A: How much is the rent?
   B: It's $1,800 a month. And you need to pay a $900 security deposit when you sign the lease.
   A: OK. Thank you.

3. A: I'm interested in the condo for rent in Canoga Park. How large is it?
   B: It's a two-bedroom with two bathrooms, so it's pretty big.
   A: Is it a good location?
   B: Yes. It's near buses and shopping.
   A: Is it bright or dark?
   B: It's very bright. It has a large bright living room. And there is a nice pool on the property.
   A: How about parking?
   B: The apartment has two parking spaces. And it's only $1,500 a month. That's cheap for this area.

4. A: I'm calling about the mobile home for rent in Topanga.
   B: Yes, it's nicely furnished and is still available.
   A: How is the kitchen in the mobile home?
   B: Very nice. It has new kitchen appliances. And it's in a nice, quiet, friendly area. You'll like it there.
   A: How much is the rent?
   B: A thousand a month. Plus a $750 security deposit.
   A: Great. I'd like to see it.

Say It *Listen to the conversation. Say it with a partner.*

A: Good morning. Water Department.
B: Hello. I'm calling because I need to turn on my water service.
A: Is this a new account?
B: Yes, it is.
A: How about tomorrow afternoon? Will you be home tomorrow afternoon?
B: Yes, tomorrow afternoon is fine.
A: OK. What's your address?

Read and Listen *Read the story. Listen to the story.*

Home

Ping is happy with her home. She lives in a two-bedroom house in a safe, quiet neighborhood. Her house has a large kitchen and a modern bathroom. There are four large windows in her living room and there is a swimming pool in her yard.

Tanya isn't happy with her apartment. There is only one bedroom. The bathroom is small and the kitchen is old. There isn't a swimming pool. And there aren't many windows. In fact, there is only one small window in her bedroom so her bedroom isn't very bright. And her neighbors are noisy.

Ping likes her home so she doesn't want to move. But Tanya isn't happy with her apartment. She wants a new place to live. She wants to be happy.

Listen and Write *Write the sentences you hear. Don't forget periods and question marks.*

1. There is a new stove in the kitchen.
2. Are there any windows in the bathroom?
3. There is a lamp on the coffee table.
4. Is there a garage?
5. There are beautiful curtains in my living room.

Pronunciation *With or questions, the voice should go up with the first choice and down with the second choice. Listen and practice the questions.*

Is it new or old?
Are they cheap or expensive?
Is it small or large?
Is the bedroom dark or bright?

CHAPTER 7: **The Community**

Page 123 (Chapter Opening, Activity 1)

Listen *Listen and repeat.*

1. a post office
2. a library
3. a bank
4. a police station
5. a movie theater
6. a supermarket
7. a drugstore
8. a gas station
9. a hospital
10. a café
11. an apartment building
12. a school
13. a fire station
14. a park

Page 123 (Chapter Opening, Activity 2)

Pronunciation

library	café
supermarket	apartment
hospital	

Page 124 (Lesson 1, Activity 1)

Say It *Listen to the conversation. Say it with a partner.*

A: Is there a post office in Tanya's new neighborhood?
B: Yes, there is.
A: Where is it?
B: It's on Third Avenue next to the library.

Page 125 (Lesson 1, Activity 4)

Say It *Listen to the conversation. Say it with a partner.*

A: Is there a hospital in this neighborhood?
B: Yes, there is.
A: Where is it?
B: It's on Tree Street. Go up Pine Street to Tree Street. Turn left on Tree Street. You can't miss it.
A: Thank you.

Page 126 (Lesson 1, Activity 5)

Listen *Listen and write the places on the map:* drugstore, supermarket, adult school, library.

1. A: Is there a drugstore in this neighborhood?
   B: Yes, there is. Where are you now?
   A: I'm at the post office.
   B: OK. Walk down Avenue B to Second Street. Turn right on Second Street. It's just past the Laundromat.
2. A: Is there a supermarket in this neighborhood?
   B: Yes, there is. Where are you now?
   A: I'm at the drugstore.
   B: OK. Walk down Avenue A to Third Street. Turn left on Third Street. You can't miss it.
3. A: Is there an adult school in this neighborhood?
   B: Yes, there is. Where are you now?
   A: I'm at the supermarket.
   B: OK. Walk along Third Street to Avenue C. Turn left on Avenue C. Go straight past Second Street to First Street. It's on the corner of First Street and Avenue C.

4. A: Is there a library in this neighborhood?
   B: Yes, there is. Where are you now?
   A: I'm at the supermarket.
   B: OK. Walk along Third Street to Avenue B. Turn left on Avenue B. It's on the right side, past the gas station.

Page 128 (Lesson 2, Activity 1)

Say It *Listen to the conversation. Say it with a partner.*

A: Where are you?
B: I'm at the library.
A: What are you doing there?
B: I'm getting an English book.
A: Oh. That's a good idea.

Page 129 (Lesson 2, Activity 3)

Say It *Listen to the conversation. Say it with a partner.*

A: Where are you going?
B: I'm going to the beauty salon.
A: Why are you going there?
B: I need to get a haircut.
A: That's a good reason.

Page 131 (Lesson 2, Activity 7)

Say It *Listen to the conversation. Say it with a partner.*

A: Excuse me. I want to go to Venice Beach. Which bus goes there?
B: Take Bus 28. The number 28 bus goes to Venice Beach.
A: Where do I get off?
B: Get off at Pacific Avenue.
A: Thanks a lot.

Page 133 (Lesson 3, Activity 1)

Say It *Listen to the conversation. Say it with a partner.*

A: Where is Tanya?
B: She's at work.
A: Where does she work?
B: She works in a clothing store. She's a salesperson.

Page 134 (Lesson 3, Activity 2)

Listen and Write *Listen to the sentences. Do you hear a place or a job or both? Write the places and jobs.*

1. A: What does your sister do?
   B: She works in a bank.
2. A: What about your husband? What does he do?
   B: He's a mechanic.
3. A: What kind of work does Jenny do?
   B: She's a cashier in a supermarket.
4. A: Where does Jeff work?
   B: He works in the café around the corner. He's a counter person.
5. A: How about Ping? What does she do?
   B: She's a receptionist.
6. A: How about you? What do you do?
   B: I'm a teacher. I work in the adult school.
   A: Do you like your job?
   B: I love it!

Page 135 (Lesson 3, Activity 4)

Say It *Listen to the conversation. Say it with a partner.*

A: What does she do?
B: She's a hair stylist.
A: What do hair stylists do?
B: They cut hair.

Page 136 (Lesson 3, Activity 6)

Pronunciation *Verbs that end in -s are pronounced three different ways: /s/, /z/, or /iz/*

Listen and repeat the verbs. Listen to the ending sound.

/s/: works, cooks, cuts
/z/: serves, gives, drives
/iz/: fixes, teaches, dances

Read the sentences in Activity 5 out loud. Practice saying the verb endings.

Page 137 (Chapter Review, Activity 1)

Read and Listen *Read the story. Listen to the story.*

Two Neighborhoods

Ping and Tanya live in different neighborhoods, but they go to the same school. Tanya walks to school. The school is right across the street from her apartment building. Ping drives to school. She lives about fifteen minutes from the school.

Tanya lives in an apartment in a very busy neighborhood. There is a park across the street from her apartment building, right behind the school. There are a lot of stores and businesses in Tanya's neighborhood. There is a post office, and there are several restaurants nearby. There is a movie theater on the next block, and there is a supermarket and drugstore near the movie theater. There is a nice café right next to her apartment building.

Ping doesn't live in an apartment. She lives in a house. There are no big buildings in Ping's neighborhood. There aren't any restaurants. There is a small grocery store a few blocks away, but there aren't any supermarkets near her home. Her neighborhood is very quiet. There is a bank one block away. But most of the buildings in Ping's neighborhood are small private homes. It isn't very busy. That's the kind of neighborhood Ping likes to live in.

Page 138 (Chapter Review, Activity 3)

Listen *Listen and write the names of the places on the map.*

1. A: Where is the bank?
   B: The bank? It's on Avenue B, right around the corner from the post office.
2. A: I'm looking for the clinic. Can you give me directions? I'm at the bank on Avenue B.
   B: Sure. Go straight along Avenue B to Third Street. Turn right on Third Street. It's in the middle of the block.

3. A: Can you tell me how to get to the drugstore from the clinic?
   B: Yes. Go out the door on Third St. Walk down Third Street to Avenue A. Turn right on Avenue A. It's near the corner of Second Street.
4. A: Is there a library nearby? I'm at the drugstore on Avenue A.
   B: Yes, there is. Just go to Second Street and turn right. It's on the right side.
5. A: I'm at the library on Second Street. Is there a supermarket nearby?
   B: Yes, there is. Walk down Second Street to Avenue A. Turn right on Avenue A. It's at the corner of First Street and Avenue A.
6. A: Is there a café in this neighborhood?
   B: Of course there is.
   A: Can I walk there from the supermarket?
   B: Yes, it's right nearby. Just walk up Avenue A to Second Street and turn left. It's right across from the library.
   A: Great. Thank you.
7. A: I'm at the café on Second Street. Is there a gas station nearby?
   B: Yes. Just go up Second Street to Avenue B and turn left. Walk down Avenue B. It's near the corner of First Street.
   A: Thank you.

Page 140 (Chapter Review, Activity 7)

Pronunciation *Listen to the ending sounds of the verbs. Write the verbs in the correct column.*

1. cuts—She cuts hair.
2. drives—He drives a bus.
3. teaches—He teaches English.
4. gives—She gives change.
5. serves—She serves lunch.
6. parks—He parks cars.
7. counts—She counts money.
8. fixes—He fixes cars.
9. dances—She dances every night.

CHAPTER 8: **Health and Safety**

Page 143 (Chapter Opening, Activity 1)

Listen *Listen and repeat.*

1. head
2. hair
3. eyes
4. nose
5. mouth
6. ears
7. neck
8. shoulder
9. arm
10. hand
11. chest
12. stomach
13. back
14. leg
15. knee
16. foot

Page 143 (Chapter Opening, Activity 2)

Pronunciation

shoulder
stomach

Page 144 (Lesson 1, Activity 1)

Say It *Listen to the conversation. Say it with a partner.*

A: What's the matter?
B: My head hurts.
A: Oh, I'm sorry to hear that.

Page 145, (Lesson 1, Activity 3)

Listen *Listen and write the parts of the body. Some are singular and some are plural.*

1. foot
2. nose
3. hair
4. hands
5. stomach
6. chest
7. knees
8. teeth
9. fingers
10. shoulder

Page 146 (Lesson 1, Activity 4)

Say It *Listen to the conversation. Say it with a partner.*

A: How are you today?
B: Not so good.
A: What's the matter?
B: My head hurts. And I have a sore throat, too.

Page 147 (Lesson 1, Activity 6)

Pronunciation *Listen and repeat the words. Stress the first syllable.*

headache   stomachache   backache
toothache   earache

Page 148 (Lesson 2, Activity 1)

Say It *Listen to the conversation. Say it with a partner.*

A: When is your appointment with Doctor Martinez?
B: It's on Monday, April 15th.
A: What time?
B: It's at eleven o'clock.
A: What room is it in?
B: It's in Room 205.

Page 148 (Lesson 2, Activity 2)

Listen *Listen to the telephone messages. Write the date, time, and place of the appointment.*

1. A: I would like to make an appointment to see Dr. Johnson.
   B: Would you like to come in tomorrow?
   A: Yes, tomorrow is good.
   B: How about 3:00?
   A: Yes, three o'clock is good.
   B: Tomorrow, Tuesday, May 8, at 3:00. Please come to Room 101.
   A: Room 101 at 3:00. OK, thank you.
2. A: Hello. I'd like to come in to see a doctor.
   B: Is it an emergency or just routine?
   A: It's not an emergency.
   B: Is next Monday all right?
   A: Yes, Monday is fine. What time?
   B: Can you come in the morning, say nine or ten o'clock?
   A: Yes. Ten o'clock is better.
   B: Monday, August 4th, at 10:00. Come to Room 600.

3. A: I need to see a doctor. Can I come in today?
   B: It's too late for today, but we can take you tomorrow.
   A: OK, what time?
   B: We open at 8:00. Come in at 8:00 and you can see the doctor right away.
   A: Where do I go?
   B: Do you have our address? 601 Rose Avenue. It's Room 100.
   A: Room 100?
   B: Friday, June 11, Room 100. What's your name?
   A: My name is…

Page 149 (Lesson 2, Activity 3)

Say It *Listen to the conversation. Say it with a partner.*

A: My daughter has a headache. What do you recommend for a headache?
B: Give her some aspirin. Aspirin is good for a headache.

Page 150 (Lesson 2, Activity 5)

Say It *Listen to the conversation. Say it with a partner.*

A: I need to make an appointment for my son. He has a bad headache.
B: Does he have a fever, too?
A: Yes, he does. He has a 103° temperature.
B: Can you bring him in at three o'clock?
A: Yes, I can.

Page 152 (Lesson 2, Activity 9)

Listen *Listen and write the missing words.*

November 15
Dear Ms. Ryan:
    I am writing this note for my son, Victor Alvarez. He is absent from school today because he is sick. He has a headache and a fever. I think he has the flu. I hope he will be back in school on Monday
Sincerely,
Norma Alvarez

Page 153 (Lesson 3, Activity 1)

Say It *Listen to the conversation. Say it with a partner.*

A: Watch out!
B: What's wrong?
A: Don't turn right there.
B: Why not?
A: The sign says, "No right turn."
B: Oh. OK.

Page 154 (Lesson 3, Activity 2)

Say It *Listen to the conversation. Say it with a partner.*

A: Emergency Operator, 911.
B: Hello, this is Eric Ryan. I want to report an emergency.
A: What is the emergency?
B: It's a car accident.
A: What is the location?
B: Main Street and Avenue B in Santa Monica.
A: OK. An ambulance is on the way.

Page 155 (Lesson 3, Activity 4)

Say It *Listen to the conversation. Say it with a partner.*

A: Hello. This is Tanya.
B: Hello, Tanya. How are you?
A: Not so good. I can't come to work today.
B: What's the matter?
A: I'm sick. I have the flu.
B: OK. I hope you feel better soon.
A: Thank you.

Page 157 (Chapter Review, Activity 1)

Read and Listen *Read the story. Listen to the story.*

Sick

"Hi, Jenny," Ping says. "Are you OK? You don't look so good."

"I don't know," Jenny says. "I think I'm sick."

"What's the matter?"

"I have a headache and body aches."

"Where does it hurt?"

"My whole body hurts. My legs hurt. My back hurts. My chest hurts. Even my hair hurts."

"Your hair hurts?"

"No, my hair doesn't really hurt. But everything else hurts and I'm tired all the time."

"Do you have a fever?" Ping puts her hand on Jenny's forehead. It feels hot. "I think you have a fever," Ping says. "You need to see a doctor. You probably have the flu."

"How about you? Do you feel OK?"

"No, I don't. I'm tired all the time, too, and I have a stomachache."

"That's terrible. Maybe we both need to go home and rest."

"Good idea. Tomorrow we both need to see a doctor."

Page 158 (Chapter Review, Activity 5)

Listen *Listen and write the sentences.*

1. My head hurts.
2. I have a headache.
3. She has a sore knee.
4. Do you have a fever?
5. Don't turn right.
6. Please step on the scale.

Page 159 (Chapter Review, Activity 8)

Pronunciation *Listen and repeat the singular and plural forms of the words.*

man	men	foot	feet
woman	women	tooth	teeth
child	children	mouse	mice

Page 160 (Chapter Review, Activity 9)

Listen *Listen and circle the word you hear.*

1. men
2. foot
3. women
4. teeth
5. child
6. mice

CHAPTER 9: **Work**

Page 163 (Chapter Opening, Activity 1)

Listen *Listen and repeat the sentences.*

1. He is an auto mechanic.
   He fixes cars.
2. She is a hair stylist.
   She cuts and styles hair.
3. He is a house painter.
   He paints houses.
4. She is a salesperson.
   She sells clothes.

Page 164 (Lesson 1, Activity 1))

Say It *Listen to the conversation. Say it with a partner.*

A: What's Julia doing?
B: She's cutting hair.
A: Why is she cutting hair?
B: It's her job. She cuts hair every day at work.

Page 165 (Lesson 1, Activity 4)

Say It *Listen to the conversation. Say it with a partner.*

A: What does he do?
B: He's a house painter. He paints houses.
A: Is he working now?
B: Yes. He's painting a house right now.

Say It *Listen to the conversation. Say it with a partner.*

A: What job skills do you have?
B: Job skills?
A: Yes, what can you do?
B: I can make clothes. I was a seamstress in my country.
A: That's a good job skill.

Pronunciation *Listen and repeat the sentences.*

When we use can, *we stress the verb after* can. *We don't stress* can.

    I can cook Chinese food.
    She can type very well.
    He can fix cars.

When we use can't, *we stress* can't *more than the verb.*

    He can't cook.
    I can't type very well.
    She can't fix cars.

Say It *Listen to the conversation. Say it with a partner.*

A: Hello. I'm calling about the office assistant position.
B: Yes. Can you type thirty words per minute?
A: Yes, I can.
B: Great. Can you come in tomorrow for an interview?
A: Yes, I can.

Say It *Listen to the conversation. Say it with a partner.*

A: Here's a job for a cashier.
B: What does it say?
A: It says ten dollars per hour.
B: What else?
A: It says "must work nights." Can you work nights?
B: Yes, I can.
A: Great. You can apply for the job.

Say It *Listen to the conversation. Say it with a partner.*

A: I'm calling about the job for an office assistant. Can you tell me about the job?
B: Yes, the pay is $14 per hour and you must type forty words per minute.
A: Oh.
B: Can you type forty words per minute?
A: No, I can't.
B: I'm sorry. You have to type forty words per minute for this job.

Say It *Listen to the conversation. Say it with a partner.*

A: What is Alison's current job?
B: She is an English teacher.
A: What was her previous job?
B: She was a teacher assistant.
A: When was she a teacher assistant?
B: She was a teacher assistant from 2003 to 2005.

Listen *Listen and write the sentences. Listen for present or past tense verbs.*

1. She was a cook in her country.
2. They were teachers.
3. He's a house painter.
4. Are you a salesperson?
5. Were they taxi drivers?
6. They are mechanics.

Say It *Listen to the conversation. Say it with a partner.*

A: What position is she applying for?
B: A salesperson position.
A: Does she want to work full time or part time?
B: She wants full time.
A: Can she work Monday to Friday?
B: Yes, she can.
A: Can she work evenings?
B: Yes, she can.
A: Can she work on Saturday and Sunday?
B: No, she can't.

Page 177 (Chapter Review, Activity 1)

Read and Listen *Read the story. Listen to the story.*

New Jobs

Some of Ping's classmates are looking for new jobs. Jenny isn't happy with her current job. She is a cashier in a café, but in Colombia she was a manager of a café. She wants to be a manager again.

Julia isn't happy with her job, either. She works in a small beauty salon in a shopping mall. But she wants to work in a big expensive salon where she can make more money. She has good skills and experience. She can cut and style hair very well. She can also color hair. Right now, she is filling out an application for a job in Beverly Hills.

Han Do wants a new job, too. He is a house painter now, but he has good office skills. He can type, file, and answer phones. And he can manage people. He was an office manager in Vietnam. He wants to work in an office again. So, he is filling out an application for a job as an office assistant.

Ping doesn't want a new job now. She wants to learn some new skills and get a good job after her baby is born. Right now, she is just thinking about having a healthy baby.

Page 178 (Chapter Review, Activity 4)

Listen *Listen and write the sentences.*

1. She answers phones and takes messages.
2. A house painter paints houses.
3. Can she cut hair?
4. He can't drive a truck.
5. What was her previous job?

Page 179 (Chapter Review, Activity 8)

Pronunciation *Listen and circle the word you hear.*

1. I can drive a truck.
2. He can't cut hair.
3. They can paint houses.
4. I can't take messages.
5. She can make clothes.
6. He can't come in tomorrow.
7. She can use a computer.
8. She can't work nights.

CHAPTER 10: **Future Plans**

Page 183 (Chapter Opening, Activity 1)

Listen *Listen and repeat.*

1. chicken
2. beef
3. rice
4. vegetables

5. fruit
6. beverages
7. dessert
8. He wants a new job.
9. She wants to see her family.
10. She wants to take a vacation.
11. He wants to start his own business.

Page 183 (Chapter Opening, Activity 2)

Pronunciation

chicken   beverages
vegetables   dessert

Page 184 (Lesson 1, Activity 1)

Say It *Listen to the conversation. Say it with a partner.*

A: We're going to have a potluck party. What do you want to bring?
B: I'm going to bring some vegetables.
A: What kind of vegetables?
B: Maybe carrots and corn.
A: That's a good idea.

Page 185 (Lesson 1, Activity 3)

Say It *Listen to the conversation. Say it with a partner.*

A: What is Marco going to bring to the party?
B: He's going to bring chicken and rice.
A: Chicken and rice?
B: Yes. That's a popular food in his country.

Page 186 (Lesson 1, Activity 5)

Listen *Listen and check your answers.*

1. apples
2. grapes
3. bananas
4. oranges
5. strawberries
6. mashed potatoes
7. lettuce
8. tomatoes
9. beans
10. milk
11. cheese
12. butter
13. bread
14. cake
15. ice cream

Page 187 (Lesson 1, Activity 8)

Say It *Listen to the conversation. Say it with a partner.*

A: What's your favorite fruit?
B: I don't know, maybe grapes or bananas. How about you?
A: My favorite fruit is…

Page 188 (Lesson 2, Activity 1)

Say It *Listen to the conversation. Say it with a partner.*

A: What are your plans for the future?
B: I want to get a better job. What are your plans?
A: I want to take a vacation.
B: That's a good idea.

Page 188 (Lesson 2, Activity 2)

Pronunciation *Listen and repeat*

The pronunciation of want to *is often reduced to* /wanna/.

    I /wanna/ get a better job.

The pronunciation of going to *is often reduced to* /gonna/.

    She's /gonna/ take a vacation.

1. I *want to* visit my family.
2. I *want to* study English.
3. I'm *going to* bring some vegetables.
4. She's *going to* bring dessert.

Page 190 (Lesson 2, Activity 7)

Say It *Listen to the conversation. Say it with a partner.*

A: I'm going to a job interview so I have to get ready.
B: What do you have to do?
A: I have to fill out an application.
B: What else?
A: I have to arrive on time. That's very important.

Page 190 (Lesson 2, Activity 8)

Listen *Listen and circle* good idea *or* bad idea.

1. The first thing I'm going to do is shake hands with the interviewer.
2. When I talk to him I'm going to try to look at his eyes.
3. I'm not going to smile because I want to look very serious.
4. I'm going to sit back and cross my legs.
5. I'm going to speak slowly and try to speak clearly.
6. I'm going to put on my sunglasses if I feel nervous so he can't see that I'm nervous.

Page 192 (Lesson 3, Activity 1)

Say It *Listen to the conversation. Say it with a partner.*

A: Good morning. Are you a new employee?
B: Yes, I am.
A: Please sign in. You have to sign in every day when you arrive.
B: OK. Thanks.

Page 193 (Lesson 3, Activity 5)

Listen *Listen and complete the class schedule for Ping.*

8:00: Arrive and hand in homework.
8:15: Study vocabulary words.
8:30: Read a story.
8:45: Listen to the story.
9:00: Answer questions about the story.
9:30: Practice speaking with a partner.

Page 197 (Chapter Review, Activity 1)

Read and Listen *Read the story. Listen to the story.*

Future Plans

Monica is going to a job interview next week. She wants to be a teacher assistant. She is going to wear a nice business suit. She is going to arrive fifteen minutes early. She is going to shake hands with the interviewer and tell about her skills and her work experience. She is going to be polite and friendly. She really wants a job as a teacher assistant.

Alison is going to have a party in her class next week. She is going to buy some paper plates and plastic cups. She is going to make a big salad and buy a pizza. She is going to ask her students to bring some popular food that people eat in their countries. Alison wants her students to have a nice good-bye party.

Ping has some interesting plans for the future. First, she is going to go to college for one semester. Then she is going to take a break from school. She is going to study at home because she is going to have a baby. She is going to stay home for a while and take care of her baby. She wants to be a good mother.

INDEX

ACADEMIC SKILLS

CULTURE TIPS

GAME TIME

LIFE SKILLS

TOPICS

WORKFORCE SKILLS